TABLE OF CONTENTS

Top 20 Test Taking Tips

1. Carefully follow all the test registration procedures
2. Know the test directions, duration, topics, question types, how many questions
3. Setup a flexible study schedule at least 3-4 weeks before test day
4. Study during the time of day you are most alert, relaxed, and stress free
5. Maximize your learning style; visual learner use visual study aids, auditory learner use auditory study aids
6. Focus on your weakest knowledge base
7. Find a study partner to review with and help clarify questions
8. Practice, practice, practice
9. Get a good night's sleep; don't try to cram the night before the test
10. Eat a well balanced meal
11. Know the exact physical location of the testing site; drive the route to the site prior to test day
12. Bring a set of ear plugs; the testing center could be noisy
13. Wear comfortable, loose fitting, layered clothing to the testing center; prepare for it to be either cold or hot during the test
14. Bring at least 2 current forms of ID to the testing center
15. Arrive to the test early; be prepared to wait and be patient
16. Eliminate the obviously wrong answer choices, then guess the first remaining choice
17. Pace yourself; don't rush, but keep working and move on if you get stuck
18. Maintain a positive attitude even if the test is going poorly
19. Keep your first answer unless you are positive it is wrong
20. Check your work, don't make a careless mistake

Core Payroll Concepts

Employee

Anyone who performs services for you is generally your employee if you can control what work is accomplished and how it is accomplished. Here is an example: Herb Falls is a salesperson who works full-time for Jack's Auto Sales. He works 6 days a week, and is in Jack's showroom on days and times that are assigned. He appraises trade-ins but they must have the sales manager's approval. Prospective customer lists belong to Jack. Herb's job includes developing leads and keeping the sales manager apprised of the results. Herb requires only minimal assistance in closing and financing sales and in other phases of his work due to his experience. He is eligible for prizes and bonuses offered by Jack in addition to his commission. Jack also pays the cost of insurance -- both health and group-term life for Herb. Under the law, Herb is Jack's employee.

Common-law employees

A worker whose services are performed under common-law rules for an employer is his or her employee if that employer controls what and how the job will be done. This is so even when the employers give the worker a free reign to do the job. Determining whether someone is an employee or independent contractor through common law rules requires examination of the business and worker. All evidence of control and independence must be considered. To determine an employee-independent contractor relationship, all information that provides proof of the degree of independence and degree of control must be taken into consideration.

Independent contractor

A payer has control of the work done by an independent contractor, and not the means and methods of finishing the job. Here is an example of an independent contractor: Sparky Watts, an electrician, submitted a job estimate to a business for electrical work at $20 per hour for 400 hours. He will receive $1,600 every 2 weeks for the next 10 weeks. This would not be considered payment by the hour. Even if Sparky works more or less than 400 hours to finish the job, he will receive $8,000. Sparky also performs additional jobs with other companies that he obtained through bids. Because of this, Watts qualifies as an independent contractor by law.

Statutory employee

Workers come under common law rules and are independent contractors by statute for certain employment tax purposes if they fall within any one of several categories. Here are some examples: 1) drivers delivering laundry or dry cleaning, vegetables, fruit, or bakery products, beverages (other than milk) or meat, if the driver is paid on commission or is your agent; 2) a life insurance sales agent who works full time and whose main business includes selling life insurance or annuity contracts, or both, mainly for one particular life insurance company; and 3) an individual who works at home on employer-supplied goods on work that is specified, and that must be returned to the employer or employer's representative.

Statutory non-employee

Statutory non-employees fall under two categories. They are real estate agents and direct sellers. Under federal tax purposes, including income and employment taxes, they are viewed as self-employed if: 1) all payments for their services as direct sellers or real estate agents are directly related to sales instead of working a certain number of hours, and 2) a written contract guides what services they perform and specifies that for federal tax purposes, they will not be treated as employees. Worker status is also addressed under a number of state laws. How the worker is paid are among the variables in different states.

Reasonable basis test

The reasonable basis test was established by the IRS to assist employers in determining whether their labor force should be treated as employees or contractors for tax purposes. The bases on which to test the status are the Judicial Precendent Safe Haven, the Past Audit Safe Haven, the Industry Practice Safe Haven, and Other Reasonable Bases.

Judicial Precedent Safe Haven refers to the taxpayer's using previous legal rulings as to whether a person was a contractor or employee (within reason). Past Audit Safe Haven refers to the taxpayer relying on an audit already executed by the IRS for employment taxes due. Industry Practice Safe Haven refers to the taxpayer relying on (within reason) recognized industry practices of a majority of industry in which he or she participates as designating a worker as a contractor. Other reasonable bases refer to the taxpayer not being able to meet Judicial Precedent Safe Haven status, Past Audit Safe Haven status, or Industry Practice Safe Haven status, but still having a reasonable basis to consider a worker a contractor.

Temporary help services and personnel

Employees are hired by temporary help services and send the workers to companies who need employees. Small businesses especially benefit from such services by getting help for shortages of a temporary nature but temporary agencies supply businesses of all sizes. Among the services offered by such agencies are payroll, bookkeeping, tax deductions, workers' compensation, and fringe benefits. Performance guarantees and fidelity bonding at no added cost are features of most national temporary personnel companies. A quick infusion of workers can come from temporary services. They may start that day or the next. A permanent employee is paid less than a temporary employee, but the costs of overtime, training, and recruiting are less, and employee downtime is reduced.

Certain factors should be considered before hiring a temporary help service including: 1) How are personnel tested and evaluated? 2) The firm with the most skilled and reliable employees is likely to have an aggressive recruiting program. 3) Does the service have a solid track record and financial stability? 4) Is the quality of work by its temporary employees checked? 5) Are personnel trained in records management, word processing, modern office methods and other important skills? All employers will not benefit from temporary services. A temporary worker may only work for six months or more for a company. It may be cheaper to pay overtime to a regular employee than using temporary personnel for jobs that require extensive supervision.

Employee leasing

Many activities similar to using temporary personnel, co-employment arrangements or professional employer organizations are involved in employee leasing, thus it can be confusing. Leasing companies are needed to provide personnel including hiring, identifying, assigning employees to the business, and skill sorting. If these workers would return to the leasing company for reassignment, then a temporary agency is basically the same thing. But if another company is used to supply the management of human resources, employee benefits, payroll, and workers' compensation for all of your workers, then this is an arrangement such as co-employment or a professional employer organization.
1

Overtime compensation with attendance bonus under the 8 and 80 system

A hospital pays an employee $12 per hour with a $100 biweekly attendance bonus under the 8 and 80 overtime system used for health care workers during a biweekly period. Here is the overtime calculation:
$100 biweekly attendance bonus
112 hours worked x $12/hour + $100 (attendance bonus) = $1,444 (total straight time compensation)
$1,444 (total straight time compensation) ÷ 112 hours = $12.89 (regular rate)
$12.89 (regular rate) x ½ = $ 6.45 (half-time premium)
$12.89 (regular rate) + $6.45 (half-time premium) = $19.34 (overtime rate)
$12.89 (regular rate) x 80 (straight time hours) = $1,031.20 (straight time earnings)
$19.34 (overtime rate) x 32 (overtime hours worked) = $ 618.88 (overtime earnings)
Total earnings for the bi-weekly period = $1,650.08.

Retention bonus using the 8 and 80 overtime system

Nurses in a hospital intensive care unit receive a $2,000 retention bonus after working six months. The retention bonus was earned over six months or 26 weeks. The weekly equivalent is $76.92 ($2,000 ÷ 26 weeks). If the employee paid under the 8 and 80 system of overtime receives the $2,000 retention bonus after six months, the employee would be due an additional $13.77 in overtime earnings after working 95 hours, 17 of which are overtime hours, in a 14-day period as follows:
$76.92 x 2 weeks = $153.84 (additional straight-time compensation)
$153.84 ÷ 95 hours worked = $1.62 (increase in regular rate)
$1.62 x ½ = $ .81 (increase in the additional half-time premium)
$ .81 x 17 hours of overtime worked = $13.77 (increase in overtime earnings due to the bonus).

Overtime compensation for working two different jobs

An employee works as a nurse's aide on a full time basis at $11 an hour. On weekends, the employee fills in as a receptionist and is paid $7 an hour. She is paid on a 40-hour workweek overtime basis. How is her overtime computed? Overtime may be computed on the regular rate of pay, determined by the weighted average of the two rates. For example, if the employee worked 40 hours at $11 and 16 hours at $7, the following is the regular rate calculation:
40 hours x $11/hour + 16 hours x $7/hour = $552 (total straight time compensation)
$552 (total straight time compensation) ÷ 56 hours worked = $9.86 (regular rate)

$9.86 (regular rate) x ½ = $4.93 (additional half time premium)
$9.86 (regular rate) + $4.93 = $14.79 (OT rate)
$9.86 (regular rate) x 40 hours = $394.40 (total straight time earnings)
$14.79 (OT rate) x 16 (OT hours) = $236.64 (total OT earnings)
Total compensation = $631.04.

Overtime for tipped employees

The law requires that an employee's regular rate of pay can never be less than the applicable minimum-wage rate. For example, a restaurant owner pays his or her tipped employees the current federal minimum wage of $7.25 per hour, which is broken down into a cash wage of $4.00 per hour and a tip credit of $3.25 per hour. The restaurant operator should calculate tipped employees' overtime rate by multiplying $7.25 (employee's regular rate of pay) by 1.5 and then subtracting the hourly tip credit of $3.25. Example: A tipped employee worked 60 hours one week. Multiply the minimum wage ($7.25 per hour) x (1.5), minus tip credit ($3.25 per hour), x number of overtime hours (20 hours), + his or her 40-hour total ($160.00) as follows:
$7.25 x 1.5 = $10.88
$10.88 - $3.25 = $7.63
$7.63 x 20 = $152.60
$152.60 + $160.00 = $312.60
The total weekly pay is $312.60.

Calculating employee's regular rate of pay

Before any kind of payroll deduction is made, the regular rate of pay is computed. The basis for regular pay is not take-home pay. In the case of those hourly employees who work a 40-hour workweek, the calculation corresponds to the hourly rate of pay that you agree to pay them and is thus, simple. When employees are not paid on an hourly basis, however, calculating the regular rate becomes more involved when employees work on a piece rate basis or are salaried. Use this formula to figure out an employee's regular rate: pay amount for a workweek/number of hours worked (not including overtime).

Biweekly rate of pay

The biweekly rate of pay of the employee is the regular rate of pay. In order to calculate the regular rate of pay, the annual salary should be divided by the number of weeks to be paid and multiplied by 2 for the biweekly rate of pay. If a worker gets only an hourly rate, the hourly rate is the regular rate. If bonuses for productivity are given, they must be included in the regular rate. If a worker gets a shift differential such as making a higher hourly pay for an unusual shift that was worked, the regular rate is still the hourly rate. Since the regular rate is simply higher because the hourly rate itself is higher with a differential, it may not be counted toward overtime pay.

Fluctuating workweek

Under the Fair Labor Standards Act (FLSA), the fluctuating workweek provides a means by which employers are legally allowed to compensate non-exempt workers for overtime worked. The fluctuating workweek, sometimes referred to as straight-time compensation, compensates the non-exempt employee with a fixed salary regardless of the hours worked, whether over or under forty hours. For the employer to utilize the fluctuating workweek, the workweek must actually fluctuate over and under forty hours, and the compensation received for the hours worked must never reduce the employee's compensation to less than minimum wage. The employer must discuss this with the employee before hiring, and the employee must agree to be compensated as such. In the event that the employee works greater than forty hours, the employer may compensate the employee by paying half his or her normal hourly rate for each hour over forty hours that he or she works.

Requirements for changing a workweek

According to the Fair Labor Standards Act, a workweek is defined as a fixed and regularly recurring 168-hour period, or seven twenty-four hour periods that occur consecutively. This period does not necessarily match the calendar week. The workweek, as defined by the Fair Labor Standards Act (FLSA) and established by an employer, is designed to determine the eligibility of employees for certain benefits and to determine compensation of overtime payments for hours worked in excess of the regular forty-hour workweek. After the employees' workweek has been established, it is to remain constant in spite of changes to the employees' work schedules. For an employer to change the workweek, he or she must abide by certain rules established under the FLSA regarding the changing of the workweek. The change initiated is to be intended to be permanent. The change may not be a regular occurrence. Additionally, the change may not be made to intentionally avoid the overtime rules established under the FLSA. If these requirements are met, the employer may change his or her definition of a regular workweek.

Compensatory time off (in lieu of overtime pay)

For an employee to receive compensatory time off in lieu of compensation, the conditions under which he or she is working must qualify under the definition of compensatory time off. Compensatory time off is defined as paid time off instead of overtime rates for overtime worked. The overtime worked must be irregular or occasional. Both exempt and non-exempt employees may be compensated in lieu of overtime with compensatory time off. Additionally, employees falling under the definition of prevailing rate employees may be compensated with compensatory time off, but there is not a requirement that they be compensated as such. This payment arrangement may also be used to compensate the above-mentioned employees in the event of required overtime accrued on flexible work schedules. The compensatory time off must be used by the employee by the end of the twenty-sixth pay period after the pay period in which the compensatory time off was earned.

Compensable time periods

Under the Fair Labor Standards Act, employers are not required to provide their employees with paid meal and rest breaks, although short breaks given while "on-the-clock" are often given to the employee as paid time. These breaks, if given, must be counted by the employer as hours worked by the employee. In the event that an employee extends this break period without the consent of the employer, the additional time is not required to be counted as hours worked, if the employer has established without question the length of the break to be taken.

Meal periods (i.e. lunch breaks) are not required under the Fair Labor Standards Act (FLSA) to be given as compensated time to the employee. However, the employee must be free from all duties associated with his or her job for the meal period to be considered bona fide. If, at any time while the employee is eating (during his or her meal period), he or she is required to perform a task for the employer, the period is not a bona fide meal period under the FLSA.

Acceptable work time rounding practices

Under the Fair Labor Standards Act, employers may use a rounding system when calculating the number of hours worked by the employee. The Fair Labor Standards Act (FLSA) allows employers to round employees' working time to the nearest quarter hour, or fifteen minutes, if they practice fair rounded techniques as defined under the FLSA. The FLSA establishes that between one and seven minutes of an hour may be rounded down, but eight to fourteen minutes must be rounded upward. It is important that the employer not always round down, as this may result in a violation of multiple parts of the FLSA. Regulation 785.48 Subpart D states that rounding is an acceptable practice, but it must not be practiced in such a manner that it fails (or is designed to fail) to fully compensate an employee for all time worked. The regulation notes that rounding addresses the issues of discrepancies in time worked compared to time shown on a time clock, but also states that major discrepancies should be avoided.

Federal minimum wage

A minimum wage for non-exempt employees is among the provisions required by the federal Fair Labor Standards Act. Effective July 2009, the minimum wage is $7.25 per hour. All qualifying non-exempt employees must be paid this rate for each hour worked during a 40-hour workweek. Beyond those 40 hours, the employee must be paid overtime at a rate of time-and-a half. A rate of $10.88 per hour is the current minimum for overtime hours. Hourly workers are not the only workers required to receive the minimum. The law requires you to pay all qualifying covered employees for a workweek an amount that is at least the minimum wage times the hours worked by an employee.

Payment for minimum-wage employees

Minimum-wage employees may be paid by the hour, by the month, by piecework, by salary, or any other way as long as it meets the minimum wage of $7.25 per hour. An employee who works 40 hours a week, for instance, must be paid at least $290. Also, cash is not the only compensation for wages. You may pay some or all of it in room and board. But that rule has exceptions: 1) the non-cash payments cannot be for profit and 2) the cost of facilities to pay your employees, if the employee is using the facility primarily for your benefit, cannot be used.

FLSA

Tests to be met
Employers are generally subject to the federal wage and hours law, the Fair Labor Standards Act (FLSA), if two tests are met. Commerce, or the scope of an employer's trade, is one test. The second, or dollar test, refers to the annual sales amounts that a business entity takes in. All employees are covered under the FLSA if all these tests are met, and

Copyright © Mometrix Media. You have been licensed one copy of this document for personal use only. Any other reproduction or redistribution is strictly prohibited. All rights reserved.

those employees must be classified under the FLSA as exempt or non-exempt. Some employees might still be individually protected by the wage and hours law even if the tests are not met.

Requirements to meet exempt status

An employer must pay an employee a salary if they are treated under FLSA as exempt. Automatically considered to be non-exempt are employees who are paid by hourly wage. However, employees who are paid by salary can be non-exempt employees as well. Exemptions from the minimum wage, equal pay, overtime pay and child labor provisions of the FLSA apply to employees such as certain home workers and those engaged in delivery of newspapers to consumers. Certain labor categories are also exempt from the minimum wage, equal pay, and overtime requirements of the FLSA (but not the child labor laws) including: seamen on non-American vessels; employees of amusement or recreational establishments having seasonal peaks; employees engaged in the fishing industry, including offshore seafood processing; certain agricultural employees; employees who are casual babysitters or companions for persons unable to care for themselves; and employees of certain weekly, semiweekly or daily newspapers of less than 4,000 circulation.

Exempt and non-exempt employees

Employers must classify all employees in their business as either exempt or non-exempt for purposes of complying with the FLSA. An employee is not entitled to the benefits and protections of the FLSA when an employee is exempt from the FLSA, and rules under the FLSA do not apply for that employee. An employer may not have to be paid minimum wage or paid under FLSA rules if the employee is exempt. An employee classified as non-exempt is entitled to provisions under the FLSA including a minimum wage, overtime pay at the rate of time and one-half the regular rate for all hours worked in excess of 40 hours per week, as well as other provisions such as equal pay and child labor protections.

Overtime requirements

There is an overtime pay requirement that mandates that employers pay non-exempt employees one and one-half times their regular rate for any hours worked in excess of 40 hours in a workweek, in addition to the minimum wage requirements of federal wage and hour laws. Employers should ensure they comply with the overtime requirements of the FLSA by: 1) making a determination of who is subject to the rules, 2) complying with overtime provisions of state law, 3) computing each worker's regular rate, and 4) understanding what composes a workweek.

Partial overtime exemptions for employees

If certain criteria are met, certain types of employees under FLSA can be partially exempt from overtime provisions. They include but are not limited to:
- retail sales employees who receive commission: commissions qualify as overtime pay if the employee's regular rate exceeds one and one-half times his statutory minimum rate and if more than one-half of the employee's compensation represents commissions
- hospital or nursing home employees: the employees may be paid overtime at one and one-half times their regular rates on the basis of a 14-day period, rather than the usual seven-day workweek, if they agreed to the arrangement prior to performance of the work and if they receive overtime pay for hours worked in excess of eight daily and in excess of 80 during the period

- law enforcement personnel including prison security personnel and firefighters.
- Union employees working under a contract with certain provisions

Workweek and compensatory time off for public sector jobs
Under the Fair Labor Standards Act, public sector employees may also be compensated with compensatory time off for overtime worked. For public sector agencies to use this compensation method, the Fair Labor Standards Act (FLSA) requires that all employees receive an hour and half of compensatory time off for each hour of overtime that they work. Law enforcement employees, seasonal activity employees, emergency responders, and firefighters are allowed to accrue up to 480 hours of compensatory time off, while other government employees are allowed to accrue 240 hours of time off before the hours must be taken. Additionally, the FLSA requires that the employees be allowed to take the time off whenever they request, unless it would severely hamper the operations of that agency. Further, the FLSA establishes guidelines for how unused compensatory time off should be paid to the employee in the event that the employee is not able to take advantage of having accrued the time off.

Following state or federal overtime rates
States have overtime provisions just as the federal government does. The guidelines under the FLSA may be more than, less than, or equal to state provisions. A general rule of thumb is that an employer must follow the state law if it is more inclusive or more generous regarding overtime pay. Even though the employer will surpass the minimum compliance requirements of the federal law, the state minimum must be followed if it is higher. If the state's overtime provisions are less demanding and the employer is subject to the federal law, then he or she must meet the federal minimum. Even if a state requires a lesser amount to be in compliance, the federal minimum must be followed.

Overtime pay for non-exempt workers
In the process of paying an employer's non-exempt workers, the employer must first determine how many hours the employee has worked. After that is completed, if there is an hourly rate for employees, one knows how much to pay: the employee's hourly rate multiplied by the number of hours up to 40, plus one and one-half times the hourly rate for the number of hours over 40. But if employees are non-exempt but are paid on some other basis and are still entitled to overtime because they worked more than 40 hours, the employer would have to figure out what their regular rates are, unless certain exceptions exist.

White-collar exemptions to wage and overtime laws
White collar exemptions (executive, administrative, and professional) under FLSA rules follow certain underlying guidelines, including duties and salary tests: 1) Salary basis and level tests -- a minimum salary is $455/week except for outside sales and certain professions such as doctors and teachers, and certain computer professionals who are paid $27.63/hour or more in straight-time pay for each hour worked, and subject to a highly compensated employee test. 2) Regardless of how much they are paid, employees who meet the exemption tests for their categories do not have to be paid overtime pay. 3) A salary alone does not make an employee exempt. 4) Generally, exempt employees are the most important, highest-ranking, or highest-skilled workers in the company. 5) A title alone does not make an employee exempt.

Administrative exemptions require the following conditions: 1) the employee's primary duty is directly related to management or general business operations and requires the exercise of independent judgment and discretion concerning significant issues; 2) the employee must work directly in assisting with the running or servicing of the business, as opposed to selling a product in a retail or service establishment or working on a manufacturing production line; 3) the employee's work is in functional areas such as accounting, finance, budgeting, auditing, insurance, labor relations, tax, quality control, purchasing, procurement, advertising, marketing, research, safety and health, personnel management, human resources, employee benefits, public relations, legal and regulatory compliance, government relations, computer network, Internet and database administration and activities that are similar.

Minimum age for employment
The minimum age for most non-agricultural work is 14 years old under child labor provisions of the Fair Labor Standards Act (FLSA). However, youth of any age may perform in radio, television, movie, or theatrical productions; deliver newspapers; perform babysitting or perform minor chores around a private home, and work in businesses owned by their parents with the exception of mining, manufacturing or hazardous jobs. Also, youth of any age may be employed to gather evergreens and make evergreen wreaths as home workers. Youth in agriculture face different age requirements. Some states may have a minimum age for employment which is higher than the FLSA. The higher minimum standard must be obeyed where both the FLSA and state child labor laws apply.

Child labor
The Fair Labor Standards Act (FLSA) is the most sweeping federal law that restricts the employment and abuse of child workers. Child labor provisions under FLSA, enforced by the U.S. Department of Labor, are designed to prohibit children's employment in jobs that are detrimental to their health and safety and to protect the educational opportunities of youth. Youth under 16 years of age have restricted hours under the FLSA as well as prohibitions on working in hazardous occupations that are too dangerous for young workers to perform.

Under FLSA standards, children under 14 years of age may not be employed in non-agricultural occupations including supermarkets and grocery stores. Employment for such children is limited to work that is exempt from the FLSA (such as delivering newspapers to the consumer and acting). Children may also perform work such as completing minor chores around private homes or casual baby-sitting, which is not covered by the FLSA. The government does not allow participation by those under 14 in the Work Experience and Career Exploration Program. This is a carefully planned work experience and career exploration program for 14 and 15-year-old youths who can benefit from a career-oriented educational program. The program is aimed at helping youths to be motivated toward education and to prepare them for the world of work.

Child labor in grocery stores
A 16 and 17-year-old may be employed under FLSA provision for unlimited hours in any occupation other than those deemed hazardous. Examples of hazardous equipment in grocery stores include certain power-driven bakery machines, power-driven meat processing machines (meat slicers, saws, patty forming machines, grinders, or choppers), commercial mixers and forklifts. Generally, no employee under 18 years of age may operate a forklift. Employees under 18 are not permitted to operate, feed, set-up, adjust, repair, or clean such machines. Minors under 18 years of age may not unload scrap paper balers or

operate paper box compactors. Under certain specific circumstances, 16 and 17-year-olds may load such machines.

Grocery stores and supermarkets may employ 14 and 15-year-olds under FLSA child labor laws, but only in certain jobs including: 1) cashiering, and the bagging and carrying out of customer orders; 2) clean up work, such as that requiring the use of vacuum cleaners and floor waxers; 3) limited cooking duties involving electric or gas grills that do not include cooking over an open flame; 4) cleaning kitchen surfaces and using non-power-driven equipment, and filtering, transporting and disposing of cooking oil, but only when the temperature of the surfaces and oils does not exceed 100ºF; and 5) shelf stocking.

Grocery stores and supermarkets may employ children who are 14 and 15- year-olds outside school hours in a variety of jobs under specified circumstances and for limited time periods. The hours and times 14 and 15-year-olds may work are limited under child labor laws to: 1) outside school hours, and on school days including Fridays, no more than 3 hours; 2) no more than 8 hours on a non-school day; 3) when school is in session, no more than 18 hours per week; 4) no more than 40 hours during a week when school is out; and 5) between the hours of 7 a.m. and 7 p.m, extended to 9 p.m. between June 1 and Labor Day.

Driving for employees 17 years of age
No employee under 18 years may serve as an outside helper on a motor vehicle under the FLSA child labor provisions. An outside helper -- who is not a driver -- is any individual whose work includes riding on a motor vehicle outside the cab for the purpose of delivering goods or assisting in transporting. If their employment is subject to the FLSA, no worker under 17 years of age may, as part of his or her job, drive a motor vehicle on public roads. As part of their employment, 17-year-olds can drive on public roads but only after meeting certain requirements related to the amount of time the 17-year-old spends driving and the weight of the vehicle.

The following requirements must be met in order for a 17-year-old to drive as part of employment: 1) the 17-year-old holds a state license valid for the type of driving involved in the job performed; 2) the 17-year-old has successfully completed a state approved driver education course and has no record of any moving violations at the time of hire; 3) the driving is limited to daylight hours; 4) the automobile or truck does not exceed 6,000 pounds gross vehicle weight; 4) the driving is only occasional and incidental to the 17-year-old's employment, such that no more than 20% of his or her work time in any workweek, and no more than one-third of his or her workday, can be spent driving; and 5) the automobile or truck is equipped with a seat belt for the driver and any passengers and seatbelt use is mandatory.

A 17-year-old may not engage in driving activities under FLSA rules as part of his or her employment that include: 1) operation of any vehicle other than a car or small truck; 2) route deliveries or route sales; 3) towing vehicles; 4) transportation for hire of passengers, property or goods; or 5) urgent, time-sensitive deliveries. Prohibited trips would include, but are not limited to, the delivery of pizzas and prepared foods to the customer and the delivery of materials under a deadline. They also may not: 6) make more than two trips away from the primary place of employment in any single day to transport passengers, other than employees of the employer, 7) drive beyond a 30-mile radius from the youth's place of employment, 8) make more than two trips away from the primary place of employment in any single day to deliver the employer's goods to a customer, or 9) provide transportation for more than three passengers.

Calculating federal income tax withholding

Percentage method

To calculate federal income tax withholding using the percentage method: 1) Determine the employee's gross wage for the payroll period. 2) Find the allowance amount from the appropriate IRS table according to the employee's frequency of payment, and multiply that amount by the number of withholding allowances claimed on the employee's Form W-4. 3) Subtract the allowance amount from the employee's gross wages to calculate the employee's taxable wage. 4) Determine the amount of federal tax using the appropriate percentage withholding table.

Here is an example of calculating federal income tax withholding by the percentage method for a bi-weekly paid employee with two personal allowances. The employee is single and has a bi-weekly gross of $1,450. 1) Determine wage: $1,450. 2) Allowance amount from IRS table for two allowances: $280.76. 3) Taxable wage ($1,450 - $280.76) = $1,169.24. 3) % withholding from bi-weekly, single table for $1,169.24 is 15% bracket ($401). 4) Tax on minimum 15% bracket = $16.80. 5) Taxable wage: $1,169.24. 5) Minus minimum amount of bracket ($1,169.24 - 401.00) = amount over minimum bracket = $768.24. 6) 15% of $768.24 = $115.24. 7) Tax on minimum amount of 15% bracket plus 15% amount over bracket minimum ($16.80 + $115.24) = $132.04 bi-weekly withholding.

Here is an example of calculating federal income tax withholding by the percentage method for a monthly paid employee with two personal allowances. The employee is married and has a monthly gross of $5,200. 1) Determine wage: $5,200. 2) Find allowance amount from IRS table for two allowances: $608.34 ($304.17 x 2). 3) Taxable wage ($5,200 - $608) = $4,592. 3) % withholding from monthly, married table for $4,592 is 15% bracket ($2,042). 4) Tax on minimum 15% bracket = $89.60) Taxable wage: $4,592. 5) Minus minimum amount of bracket ($4,592 - 2,042 = amount over minimum bracket = $2,550. 6) 15% of $2,550 = $382.50. 7). Tax on minimum amount of 15% bracket plus 15% amount over bracket minimum ($89.60 + $382.50) = $472.10 monthly withholding.

Wage brackets

Here is an example of calculating withholding for federal income tax using wage brackets: A married employee is paid $4,750 gross each month. The employee has $800 of tax deferred deductions. This employee has in effect a Form W-4 claiming single marital status and 3 withholding allowances. The federal income tax is calculated as follows: Gross earnings: 1) $4,750 - $800 deferred deductions. 2) Taxable income: $3,950. 3) Allowances on W-4: 3. 4) Determine pay cycle: monthly. 5) Marital status on W-4: Single. 8) Tax table, single, monthly payroll. 9) Find appropriate range by comparing $3,950 to tax table ranges for single, monthly payroll, (the income of $3,950 is between the range of $3,920 but not over $3,960). According to the table, the tax on $3,950 is $363.

Manual calculations

Several infrequently used ways for computing tax withholding can be used with manual calculations. They include: 1) annualized wages; compute the employee's annual pay rate and then figure the annual withholding amount in the IRS Annual Payroll Period tax table. Divide the amount by the number of pay periods in the year to determine the deduction for an individual paycheck. 2) Partial-year employment can be used as a basis only at an employee's written request. The request must contain certain information, including a statement that the employee anticipates working for all employers during the calendar year for no more than 245 days in total. The company determines pay periods and tables to calculate the withholding. 3) Year-to-date wages which are cumulative can be used as a basis, also with written requests. Year-to-date wages are calculated and percentage methods are used for figuring withholding.

Withholding for supplemental pay

An employee may have a large payment earlier in the year maybe due to a bonus or commission. The extra payment is generally added to the employee's regular pay, putting the employee into a higher tax bracket and causing a withholding that is larger than necessary at the end of the year (the employee will receive a tax refund). One way to avoid such excessive tax withholdings is to separate the supplemental pay from the base pay and issue two separate payments to an employee. The percentage withheld under this method will likely be smaller than if the pay had been combined into one paycheck. Another method that can be used is to withhold a flat 25 percent of the combined amount. The first method is usually easier for computerized systems.

Computation of employee Medicare taxes

Employers must withhold 1.45% of each employee's pay for Medicare. The employer is required to match this amount, so the total amount sent to the government is 2.9%. There is no upper limit on the amount of withholding, which applies to all earnings the employee has throughout the year. Here is an example: Victory Computer salesperson, Sylvia Bacon, has an annual base pay of $25,000. Her commissions and performance bonuses totaled $150,000 for the past year. That gave her a total compensation of $175,000. The combined amount that Sylvia and Victory Computer will submit to the government for Medicare is as follows:
Total annual pay $175,000
Total annual pay subject to the
Medicare tax $175,000
Tax rate 2.9%
Medicare taxes to be remitted $5,075

Computation of Additional Medicare Tax

The Additional Medicare Tax is a tax imposed to fund the Affordable Care Act. It is a 0.9% tax applied to all Medicare wages earned beyond a particular threshold based on the individual's filing status: $250,000 for married filing jointly, $125,000 for married filing separately, and $200,000 for all others. This is imposed in addition to the 1.45% ordinary Medicare tax upon all wages. Unlike ordinary Medicare taxes which have both an employee and employer portion, the Additional Medicare Tax is solely an employee liability, yet it remains the employer's obligation to withhold the tax and remit it to the government. Although the tax calculation depends upon an employee's filing status, employers are legally required to always withhold the 0.9% tax on any Medicare wages an employee earns above $200,000 with that employer, even if the employee requests a different, more accurate withholding.

Consider this example: a husband's Medicare wages are $220,000, and his wife's are $25,000. The employer should withhold $20,000 x 0.9% = $180 on his wages. Assuming this couple would file jointly, their joint income ($245,000) would be below the required threshold of $250,000, and hence they could claim this $180 back as an overpayment.

Computation of employee Social Security taxes

Employers must withhold 6.2% of each employee's pay for Social Security. The employer must match that amount for a total of 12.4% that goes to the government. The withholding applies to the first $118,500 (2016) of employee pay in each calendar year. This number is regularly increased by Congress. Here is an example: Sharon Ennis is the vice president of Westminster Savings and Loan. She earned $160,000 in calendar year 2015. She expects to be paid the same amount in 2016, and wants to know how much Social Security tax will be deducted from her pay in that year. The calculation is as follows:
- Total annual pay: $160,000
- Total annual pay subject to the Social Security tax: $118,500 (2016)
- Tax rate: 6.2%
- Social Security taxes to be withheld: $7,347.00

Backup withholding

The term backup withholding describes the requirement by the IRS of the withholding of taxes on certain type of income if the payee does not provide his or her Social Security number, or other identifying number. The backup withholding rate is 28%. The types of income subject to backup withholding are rents, royalties, dividends, interest, patronage dividends, commissions and fees paid to independent contractors, payments from brokers on transactions, and payments from fishing boat operators. Most United States citizens and legal resident aliens are exempt from backup withholding. The situations under which citizens and resident aliens are not exempt from backup withholding are: not providing an identifying number in a timely manner, the IRS informs the payer that the identify number is not correct, underreporting of interest and/or dividends (after the IRS attempts to contact the recipient over a period of four months), and failure to certify that one is not subject to backup withholding (identified on form W-9).

Social security requirements for public-sector workers

When the Social Security system was enacted in 1935, it specifically excluded public sector employees. Instead, government employees contributed to the Civil Service Retirement System, or CSRS. In 1951, Congress added section 218 to the law allowing states to provide optional coverage under the Social Security system to state government employees. This meant that the employee had to begin contributing to the Social Security system. This optional coverage, however, also meant that the government workers could opt out of the coverage. In 1984, federal employees were allowed to begin contributing to the Federal Employees Retirement System, or FERS. With the advent of FERS, CSRS contributors were allowed to switch to FERS, but if they did not, they would be required to pay into Medicare.

Public Sector employees generally have the option to opt out of contributing to Social Security. If they do, they are likely to not qualify for Social Security benefits unless they receive them for a reason other than contributing, such as spousal benefits. If they do qualify, their benefit may be reduced.

Payment of FUTA

The Federal Unemployment Tax (FUTA) is paid only by employers. It is set at 6.0% of the first $7,000 an employee earns in a year. (Prior to July 1, 2011, this rate was 6.2%.) Amounts paid will generally be lower because employers get credits that are based on the money they pay into state unemployment programs. The credit claimed cannot exceed 5.4%. Whenever the maximum credit is applied against the federal rate, the effective rate will fall to 0.6%.

The amount of Federal Unemployment Tax that is owed must be computed at the end of each calendar quarter, after which the taxes must then be deposited. Because of the wage ceiling, most FUTA taxes will be paid in the first quarter, with the remainder falling into the second quarter.

FUTA taxes are not payable in situations such as: 1) a household employer who pays cash wages totaling less than $1,000 for all household employees in a calendar quarter for household employees (as defined by the Form 940 instructions); or 2) an agricultural employer who pays cash wages of less than $20,000 to farm workers in a calendar quarter, or employs less than 10 farm workers during at least some part of a day during any 20 or more different weeks during the year. FUTA tax does not apply to non-cash payments, expense reimbursements, or various disability payments; or to amounts paid full-commission insurance agents or non-employees (such as contractors or consultants); and to several other limited situations.

Common errors by employers reporting Social Security taxes

Common errors by employers reporting Social Security include: 1) Reports received with erroneous Employer Identification Numbers (EINs). Since Social Security Administration (SSA) and IRS maintain employer records by EIN, amounts reported may be credited to the wrong record. Missing or incorrect EINs may result in IRS assessing penalties. 2) Incorrect employee names and Social Security numbers (SSN). To properly credit reported earnings, SSA must match the employee name and Social Security number on the wage report to the name and number in SSA's files. 3) Wage Reports for Years After Employee's Death. Payments made on behalf of a deceased employee in the year after the employee died cannot be credited as wages for Social Security purposes.

Federal compliance requirements for new-hire documentation and for remitting withholding and payroll taxes

Employers must verify that each new employee is legally eligible to work in the United States. Employers must have employees fill out Form I-9, Employment Eligibility Verification and Form W-4, Employee's Withholding Allowance Certificate. If they qualify for and want to receive advanced earned income credit payments, they must give you a completed Form W-5, Earned Income Credit Advanced Payment Certificate. Employees must get each employee's name and Social Security Number (SSN) and enter them on Form W-2. Employers must deposit income tax withheld and both the employer and employee Social Security and Medicare taxes (minus any advance EIC payments) on either a monthly or semiweekly period, as determined by a review of the Form 941 (or Form 944 for annual filers) submissions during a prescribed lookback period. Employers can make deposits either electronically, using the Electronic Federal Tax Payment System, or by taking their deposit and Form 8109-B, Federal Tax Deposit Coupon to an authorized financial institution or a Federal Reserve bank serving their area.

Reporting elective deferrals and designated Roth contributions to a 401 (k) plan

Here is an example of reporting elective deferrals and designated Roth contributions to a 401 (k) plan: For 2016, Employee A (age 45) elected to defer $18,300 to a section 401(k) plan, made a designated Roth contribution of $1,000 to the plan, and made a voluntary (non-Roth) after-tax contribution of $600. Additionally, the employer made a qualified nonelective contribution of $2,000 to the plan and a nonelective profit-sharing employer contribution of $3,000. The total elective deferral of $18,300 is reported in box 12 with code D (D 18300.00) and the designated Roth contribution is reported in box 12 with code AA (AA 1000.00). The return of excess salary deferrals and excess designated Roth contributions, including earnings on both, is reported on Form 1099-R.The $600 voluntary after-tax contribution may be reported in box 14 (this is optional) but not in box 12. The $2,000 nonelective contribution and the $3,000 nonelective profit-sharing employer contribution may be reported in box 14.

Form I-9

The purpose of the Form I-9, *Employment Eligibility Verification*, as required by the U.S. Citizenship and Immigration Service (USCIS) is to verify that a prospective employee is authorized to work in the United States. The form serves as the documentation that the employee has presented the acceptable number and types of verification documents to the employer. All employees, whether citizens or legal aliens, are required to complete this form if they were hired after November 6, 1986. The form consists of three sections:
- Section 1, Employee – Attestation of citizenship status
- Section 2, Employer – Attestation of documents which were verified
- Section 3, Employer – Re-verification (if required) of documents

Documents to identify prospective employees

An employer must verify the identity of a prospective employee, using one of a combination of the types of documents listed on the form.

List A Documents:
1. U.S. Passport or Passport Card
2. Permanent Resident Card or Alien Registration Receipt Card
3. Foreign passport that contains a temporary I-551 stamp or notation
4. Employment Authorization Document (Form I-766)

List B Documents:
1. Driver license or ID card issued by a state
2. ID card issued by federal, state or local government agencies
3. School ID card with a photograph
4. Voter Registration card

List C Document:
1. Social Security card (that does not indicate not authorized to work)
2. Certification of Birth Abroad (Form FS-545)

3. Certification of Report of Birth (Form DS-1350)
4. Original or certified copy of birth certificate issued by a state

Form SS-4

The purpose of Form SS-4, *Application for Employer Identification Number*, is to apply for issuance of an Employer Identification Number (EIN) for a sole proprietorship, corporation, partnership, estate, trust and other entities. An EIN effectively establishes a business tax account for the entity and is valid only for business use, not for personal use. Entities or authorized representatives may file the form by telephone, fax, on-line or by mail with the Internal Revenue Service. If the EIN is not received prior to the due date for the first tax payment, the words "applied for" may be used on the first return.

EIN and SSN

An Employer Identification Number (EIN) is a nine-digit number (in the format 12-3456789) intended for use by entities engaged in a trade or business for purposes of filing returns and paying taxes resulting from the trade or business. A Social Security Number (SSN) is an nine-digit number (in the format 123-45-6789) assigned to an individual for purposes of recording earnings as an employee and subsequently verifying eligibility for receipt of retirement or disability benefits.

Form SS-5

The purpose of Form SS-5, *Application for a Social Security Card*, is for an individual to apply for a Social Security Number. The form is used to apply for a new card or a replacement card or to make changes to the information on an existing card. The application and evidence documents can be filed by mail or presented in person at any social security office. If mail is used, evidence documents will be returned by mail after the application process is completed.

The four types of documents are as follows:
- Age – hospital or religious (if before age of 5) record of birth or passport or final adoption decree.
- Identity – driver license, immigration document, life insurance policy, court ordered name change, final adoption decree, marriage/divorce records, military ID card, passport, employee ID card, U.S. State card, Foreign ID card.
- U.S. Citizenship – birth certificate, Consular Report of Birth, passport, Certificate of Citizenship, Certificate of Naturalization.
- Immigration Status – If not a citizen, an immigration status document from the Department of Homeland Security (DHS) such as I-551, I-94, I-688B or I-766.

Form SS-8

The purpose of Form SS-8, *Determination of Worker Status for Purposes of Federal Employment Taxes and Income Tax Withholding*, is to request from the Internal Revenue Service (IRS), a clarification of the status of a worker regarding eligibility for or applicability of federal employment taxes and income tax withholding. A determination so requested is only applicable to federal tax matters and is not to be construed as a determination regarding proposed or hypothetical situations. The form must be filed with the appropriate

Internal Revenue Service (IRS) office in original form, signed by the taxpayer, or officer if a corporation.

Determination letter and information letter

A determination letter represents a formal decision or finding regarding an employee, is applicable only to that employee, and is binding upon the Internal Revenue Service (IRS). An information letter may be issued in lieu of a determination letter and as such, is not binding upon the IRS. It is intended to be advisory in nature and provide guidance to the affected employee regarding satisfaction of federal tax obligations.

Form W-2

The purpose of Form W-2, *Wage and Tax Statement*, is for an employer to report to each employee who earned income in the tax year, information regarding the amount of earnings and amount of income, social security and Medicare taxes withheld for that year. Every employer engaged in a trade or business must report for, and to, all employees and also report the same information to the Social Security Administration (SSA) and city, state or local tax agency.

Copies

There are six copies of Form W-2 as follows:
1. Copy A – Provided to the Social Security Administration
2. Copy B – Provided to the Employee (for federal tax return)
3. Copy C – Provided to the Employee (for employee record)
4. Copy D – Retained by the Employer
5. Copy 1 – Provided to the City, State or Local Tax Agency
6. Copy 2 – Provided to the Employee (for employee state or local tax return)

Form W-2C

The purpose of Form W-2C, *Corrected Wage and Tax Statement*, is to correct errors on previously issued Form W-2 filed with the Social Security Administration and/or distributed to an employee. It is not to be used to report corrections to back pay nor to report corrections to gambling winnings (Form W-2G). A Form W2-C, *Corrected Wage and Tax Statement*, need not be filed with the SSA in order to correct the address for an employee if all other information on the previously filed Form W-2 was correct. However, a revised Form W-2 or W-2C must be issued to the employee containing the correct address. It should be labeled as a Reissued Statement. No filings are necessary with the SSA.

Form W-3

The purpose of Form W-3, *Transmittal of Wage and Tax Statements*, is to summarize the transmittal of paper copies of Form W-2, copy A to the Social Security Administration (SSA). Form W-3 is to be used only in conjunction with the underlying Forms W-2, even if only a single W-2 is filed. Form W-3 is never to be filed without the corresponding Forms W-2. If the employer chooses to file Form W-2 information electronically, Form W-3 is not required.

<u>Reconciliation requirements</u>
Since Form W-3, *Transmittal of Wage and Tax Statements* is a document intended to summarize the amounts reported in each corresponding Form W-2, these summary amounts must agree to the related employment tax returns. The forms to which the W-3 must be reconciled are Form 941, *Employer's Quarterly Federal Tax Return*, Form 941-SS, *Employer's Quarterly Federal Tax Return – Social Security and Medicare*, Form 943, *Employer's Annual Federal Tax Return for Agricultural Employees*, and Form 944, *Employer's Annual Federal Tax Return*.

Form W-3C

Form W-3C, *Transmittal of Corrected Wage and Tax Statements,* is to be used in conjunction with Form W-2C for the transmittal of reissued and corrected paper Forms W-2, copy A to the Social Security Agency (SSA). Form W-3C must be used even if only a single Form W-2 is reissued. A separate Form W-3C is required for each combination of tax year, form and kind of payer/employer. If the employer chooses to file Forms W-2 and W-2C electronically, Form W-3C is not required.

Form W-4

The purpose of Form W-4, *Employee's Withholding Allowance Certificate*, is for the employee to document the amount of federal tax withholding to be withheld by an employer. The form requires that the amount of withholding be determined based upon the number of allowances plus any additional dollar amount desired. The form does not allow for percentages to be applied to income for withholding purposes. The Personal Allowances Worksheet section is provided solely for to assist the taxpayer in determining the appropriate number of allowances. Using the form is voluntary; it is not required to be filed.

Using Form W-9, *Employee's Withholding Allowance Certificate,* an employee may claim an exempt status if the following two conditions are met:
- The employee had no federal tax liability in the previous year and was entitled to a full refund of any amounts withheld, and
- The employee expects to have a zero tax liability in the current year.

However, even if the above two conditions are met, the employee is not entitled to an exempt status if the following two conditions apply:
- The amount of income of the employee exceeds $1,000 of which $350 is unearned income, and
- The employee is eligible to be claimed as a dependent on the tax return of another person.

Form W-4P

The purpose of Form W-4P, *Withholding Certificate for Pension or Annuity Payments*, is for pensioners and annuitants to document to the payer the amount of funds to be withheld for federal income tax purposes. This form is also used to indicate a zero withholding amount. The Personal Allowances Worksheet section is provided solely for to assist the taxpayer in determining the appropriate number of allowances for periodic payments. Using the form is voluntary; it is not required to be filed. Withholding for payments that are not periodic (i.e.

one-time or lump sum), is required to be at least 10% of the amount paid unless an election not to withhold is made.

If a Form W-4P is not provided, the payer is required to withhold as follows:
- For periodic payments: the amount of withholding as if the payer claimed a status of married with three withholding allowances.
- For nonperiodic payments: 10% of the total amount payable.

Form W-4S

The purpose of Form W-4S, *Request for Federal Income Tax Withholding From Sick Pay*, is to document to a third party payer (as opposed to an employer) the amount of funds to be withheld for federal income tax purposes. It is important to note that withholding is not required; the form is provided for those individuals who desire a withholding amount.

For purposes of this form, sick pay is defined as:
- A payment received under the terms of a plan to which the employer is a party, and,
- A payment in lieu of wages for a temporary period of absence from work due to injury or illness.

Form W-9

The purpose of Form W-9, *Request for Taxpayer Identification Number (TIN) and Certification*, is for a payer to obtain the correct identification number of a taxpayer in order to complete and information return to the Internal Revenue Service (IRS). Such items to be reported by the payer include income paid to the taxpayer, real estate transactions, mortgage interest paid by the taxpayer, acquisition or abandonment of secured property by the taxpayer, cancellation of debt to the taxpayer and contributions to an IRA by a taxpayer.

Back-up withholding

Back-up withholding is the requirement of a payer by the Internal Revenue Service (IRS) to withhold a portion of certain payments and remit same to the IRS. Payments that may be subject to such withholding include the following:
- Interest
- Tax-exempt interest
- Dividends
- Broker/Barter exchange transactions
- Rents
- Royalties
- Nonemployee pay
- Certain payments from fishing boat operators

Form 843

The purpose of Form 843, *Claim for Refund and Request for Abatement*, is to request that a refund or an abatement be granted for certain taxes, penalties, interest, fees and some additions to taxes previously paid. In general, Form 843 is to be used whenever the amendment version of a specific form (typically the form number followed by an X) does not exist. For example, a tax paid using Form 1040 can only be refunded or abated using form 1040X. Form 843, *Claim for Refund and Request for Abatement*, cannot be used by taxpayers to abate income, estate or gift taxes, nor can it be used by employers to abate FICA, RRTA or income tax withholdings. In addition, a refund or abatement of any tax that uses a form that includes a specific version for amendments (the so-called X version) cannot be claimed using Form 843.

Form 940

The purpose of Form 940, *Employer's Annual Federal Unemployment (FUTA) Tax Return*, is to report the annual federal unemployment tax liability for employers, subject to the Federal Unemployment Tax Act (FUTA). The liability amount is based on a percentage of the first $7,000 in wages paid to each employee during each calendar year. FUTA is a tax paid solely by employers; no amounts are withheld from employees. FUTA taxes are in addition to any amounts levied by a state.

Employers are subject to the Form 940, *Employer's Annual Federal Unemployment (FUTA) Tax Return* filing requirement if either of the following two scenarios is present:
- Total wages of at least $1,500 were paid to all employees during any calendar quarter of the current of previous years, or
- One or more employees worked at least part of any day in at least 20 weeks of either the current or previous year.

It is important to note that special rules apply for employers of:
- Household employees
- Agricultural employees
- Indian tribal government employees
- Tax-exempt organization employees
- State or local government employees

Form 941

The purpose of Form 941, *Employer's Quarterly Federal Tax Return*, is to report by employers to the Internal Revenue Service (IRS) the total amount of wages paid, income taxes withheld and social security and Medicare taxes due (both employee and employer portions). Employers who make a previous election with the IRS may also use Form 941 rather than Form 944 for annual filing purposes. It is important to note that Form 941 is not applicable to report either back-up withholding or federal income tax withholding on payments which are considered to be nonpayroll in nature (i.e. pensions, annuities and gambling winnings). Such amounts must be reported using Form 945, Annual *Return of Withheld Federal Income Tax*. The six types of payments which must be included on Form 941, *Employer's Quarterly Federal Tax Return* are as follows:
- Wages paid
- Tips received by employees
- Federal income tax withheld
- Employer and employee share of social security and Medicare taxes due
- Adjustments for fractions of cents to certain taxes
- COBRA premium assistance payment credits

Form 941X

The purpose of Form 941X, *Adjusted Employer's Quarterly Federal Tax Return or Claim for Refund,* is to amend amounts previously reported on a Form 941, *Employer's Quarterly Federal Tax Return,* including any requests for refund. However, if a refund is requested for previously assessed interest and/or penalties, Form 843, *Claim for Refund and Request for Abatement* is to be used instead. The income and tax items that can be corrected using Form 941-X include the following:
- Wages, tips and other compensation and income taxes withheld from each
- Taxable social security wages and tips
- Taxable Medicare wages and tips
- Advance earned income credit (EIC) payments (prior to 1/1/2011)
- Credits for COBRA premium assistance payments
- Credits for and exemptions from employer's share of qualified social security tax

Form 943

The purpose of Form 943, *Employer's Annual Federal Tax Return for Agricultural Employees*, is to report by an employer to the Internal Revenue Service (IRS), wages paid, income tax withheld and the employer and employee portions of social security and Medicare taxes due for agricultural employees (farmworkers). It is important to note that household workers in a private resident are not considered to be agricultural employees. Withholding is required on all cash wages paid to agricultural workers that meets either of the following two criteria:
- Any employee is paid no less than $150 in a year, or
- The total wages paid to all employees no less than $2,500.

Compensation paid to H-2A visa holders

Compensation paid to agricultural workers who entered the country using an H-2A visa is not subject to social security and Medicare taxes, neither for employee withholding nor for employer match. In addition, federal income tax is not required to be withheld for H-2A visa holders unless voluntarily requested by the employee. If no less than $600 is paid to all workers who hold an H-2A visa, the total amount paid is reported separately from the amounts paid of all other agricultural workers.

Form 944

The purpose of Form 944, *Employer's Annual Federal Tax Return*, is to report to the Internal Revenue Service (IRS) by so-called small employers (those with a combined annual liability for income, social security and Medicare taxes of no more than $1,000) the wages paid, federal income taxes withheld and employer and employee share of social security and Medicare taxes due. This return is filed once annually, rather than quarterly as for larger employers. Form 944 is used in lieu of the Form 941 series for reporting the following items:
- Wages paid
- Tips received by employees
- Federal income tax withheld
- Employer and employee share of social security and Medicare

- Various current year adjustments
- Credits for COBRA premium assistance payments

Employers who are ineligible to file Form 944, *Employer's Annual Federal Tax Return,* are follows:
- Employers to whom an Internal Revenue Service (IRS) notification to file annually was not issued.
- Employers of household employees.
- Employers of agricultural employees.

Form 945

The purpose of Form 945, *Annual Return of Withheld Federal Income Tax,* is for payers to report to the Internal Revenue Service (IRS) the amount of federal income tax withheld on the following types of payments:
- Pensions
- Military retirement
- Indian gaming profits
- Voluntary withholding of certain government payments
- Back-up withholding

Form 1042

The purpose of Form 1042, *Annual Withholding Tax Return for U.S. Source Income of Foreign Persons,* is for employers to report to the Internal Revenue Service (IRS) the amount of income tax withheld on certain income paid to nonresident aliens, foreign partnerships, foreign corporations, foreign estates and foreign trusts. In addition, any amounts paid subject to the 2% excise tax on certain federal procurement payments is also reported. Form 1042 must be filed in any of the following criteria are met:
- Form 1042-S is required to be filed, or
- Gross investment income is paid to taxable foreign private foundations, or
- Specified federal procurement payments are paid to any foreign person

Form 1042-S

The purpose of Form 1042-S, *Foreign Person's U.S. Source Income Subject to Withholding,* is to report all income subject to withholding for foreign persons such as nonresident aliens, foreign partnerships, foreign corporations, foreign estates and foreign trusts. In general, the income subject to withholding includes periodic payments (such as interest, rents and royalties, among others), certain natural resource gains and certain gains on certain intellectual property.

Form 1042-T

The purpose of Form 1042-T, *Annual Summary and Transmittal of Forms 1042-S,* is to summarize the income and taxes withheld amounts from all corresponding Forms 1042-S (*Foreign Person's U.S. Source Income Subject to Withholding).* Both forms are transmitted (delivered) to the Internal Revenue Service (IRS) in paper form. It is important to note that if more than 250 Forms 1042-S are to be filed, the filing must be electronic, in which case Form 1042-T is not used.

Form 1096

Form 1096, *Annual Summary and Transmittal of U.S. Information Returns*, is used to summarize each type of information return that is to be transmitted (delivered) to the Internal Revenue Service (IRS) in paper form. A separate Form 1096 must be used for each information return group. For example, if Forms 1097, 1098 and 1099 are to be filed, a separate 1096 is required for each (total of three). It is important to note that if more than 250 such information returns are to be filed, the filing must be electronic, in which case Form 1096 is not used.

Form 1099-R

Form 1099-R, *Distributions From Pensions, Annuities, Retirement or Profit-Sharing Plans, IRAs, Insurance Contracts, etc.*, is to report to a recipient and the Internal Revenue Service (IRS), by a payer, amounts paid to and federal income taxes withheld from a recipient related to various distributions no less than $10 including the following:
- Profit-sharing or retirement plans
- Individual retirement arrangements (IRA)
- Annuities
- Pensions
- Insurance contracts
- Survivor income benefit plans
- Disability payments
- Charitable gift annuities

Form 1099-MISC

The purpose of Form 1099-MISC, *Miscellaneous Income*, is to report to each recipient and the Internal Revenue Service (IRS), by a payer, certain amounts paid to and federal income taxes withheld from each recipient. Payments that are reportable are only those in the course of a trade or business. Personal payments are not included. Form 1099-MISC is also used to report any amounts withheld under the federal back-up withholding requirements. The types of payments which must be reported using Form 1099-MISC, *Miscellaneous Income* are as follows:
- Royalties no less than $10
- Payments totaling no less than $600 for items including but not limited to:
    - Rents
    - Services
    - Prizes and awards
    - Other income payments
- Any fishing boat proceeds
- Payments to an attorney no less than $600

Form 8233

The purpose of Form 8233, *Exemption From Withholding on Compensation for Independent (and Certain Dependent) Personal Services of a Nonresident Alien Individual*, is to claim an exemption (based upon tax treaty) from the withholding requirements for independent personal services, including any amounts received for scholarship or fellowship income that is not classified as compensatory. The definition of nonresident alien for purposes of Form 8233, *Exemption From Withholding on Compensation for Independent (and Certain Dependent) Personal Services of a Nonresident Alien Individual,* is any noncitizen who does not qualify as a resident alien. A resident alien is one who meets the requirements of either the green card test or the substantial presence test.

Withholding agent

A withholding agent is deemed to be any person or entity that is required to withhold tax such as an individual, trust, estate, partnership, corporation, government agency, nominee, association or tax-exempt foundation. It is the withholding agent who bears ultimate responsibility for the taxes that are required to be withheld. An agent who does not withhold for an entity that does not satisfy the taxes due is assigned responsibility for the amounts to be paid.

Maintaining confidentiality over payroll records

The nature of payroll is to use personal compensation and taxation information, as well as certain life choice and event information in order to administer the function of paying employees and managing tax withholdings. Because this information is highly personal to each individual employee, public disclosure is neither advisable nor appreciated. In addition, employers may face certain liability for the unauthorized disclosure of personal information. Such liability may be to legal actions by an aggrieved employee, or in violation of federal and state laws preventing such disclosure. For example, records relating to medical conditions or histories of employees and families are mandated to be confidential by the Family and Medical Leave Act (FMLA). In addition, the Health Insurance and Portability Act (HIPAA) also prohibits disclosure of individually identifiable medical information in all cases other than those conditions authorized by the act.

Breach of confidentiality

Examples of a breach in the confidentiality of employee records include, but are not limited to, the following:
- Disclosure of rate of pay and deduction information of an employee.
- Disclosure of the presence of a medical condition of an employee to a person not authorized by the employee or as per the HIPAA permitted disclosure list.
- Medical information retained as per the FMLA of an employee to a person other than,
  - The supervisor of an employee.
  - First aid and safety personnel regarding potential emergency treatment.
  - FMLA government investigative personnel.

Resources for federal income and employment tax regulations

The five primary resources available for guidance on federal income and employment tax regulations are as follows:
- The Congressional Record – printed daily containing all activities of the Senate and House of Representatives
- The Federal Register – contains proposed, temporary and final regulations that are issued by an agency of the federal government.
- Internal Revenue Bulletin – contains recently issued regulations, rulings, procedures, etc. from the Internal Revenue Service (IRS).
- Cumulative Bulletins – hardcover editions containing all bulletin information issued for a year.
- SSA/IRS Reporter – contains wage and hour and employment tax information as published by the Social Security Administration (SSA) and the Internal Revenue Service (IRS).

The Internal Revenue Service (IRS) also provides the following sources of tax guidance for employers:
- Revenue Procedures – official statements regarding the proper manner of tax compliance for various issues.
- Revenue Rulings – official interpretation of the application of a statute to a given set of facts and circumstances.
- Private Letter Rulings – a revenue ruling requested by a specific taxpayer and therefore applicable only to that taxpayer.
- Publications – guidance for taxpayers regarding specific requirements of tax laws.
- Internal Legal Opinions – internal documents including Service Center Advice, Field Service Advice and Internal Legal Memoranda.
- Announcements – ad hoc publication of informational and guidance information.

Payroll Professionals Tax Center

The Payroll Professionals Tax Center at IRS.gov has information that includes the following:
- Employment taxes, deposit and reporting rules
- Recent legislation
- Employer information for seasonal and part-time employees
- Tax forms and publications
- Information and guidance for reporting agents
- Worker classification issues
- Information on electronic options

Regulatory standards applied by payroll services

In addition to tax and employment laws, payroll services must also administer requirements that include wages, hours worked, garnishments, child support, discrimination, family leave, immigration and escheatment. These and other requirements are promulgated by various employment related laws including, but not limited to, the following:
- Social Security Act
- Family and Medical Leave Act

- Americans With Disabilities Act
- Civil Rights Act
- Immigration and Control Act
- Age Discrimination in Employment Act

Shared services environment

A shared services environment is an organization serving one or multiple entities that provides common administrative services. Examples include the functions of accounting, customer service, credit and collections and information technology. In a payroll context, a shared service environment is one in which the services provided to employees are centralized for one or more entities. The objective is to improve the service offering to the employees as well as rationalize the cost of services to the employers, using best industry practices and service level metrics. From an employee perspective, a shared service environment is intended to provide a single point of contact from which an employee can receive information or resolve issues using customer service employees trained and empowered to provide such services. From an employer perspective, a shared service environment is intended to standardize business processes in compliance with company policies and procedures and achieve efficiencies via economies of scale. The net result of a successful environment is the delivery of a higher level of customer satisfaction via increased responsiveness and accuracy, all at a lower cost.

Sarbanes-Oxley (SOX) rules

General requirements
The Sarbanes-Oxley Act of 2002 was intended to enhance existing securities regulation in order to mitigate fraudulent accounting practices by public companies. The Act, known as SOX, has a number of provisions but is popularly known for the following two key requirements:
- Certification, under penalty of criminal action, the accuracy of the financial statements of a company by certain officers.
- A requirement that the internal controls and related business processes of a company be documented and certified as accurate by a registered public accounting firm.

Compliance requirements for a payroll operation
The key effect of the Sarbanes-Oxley rules (SOX) on a payroll operation is the heightened requirement for well-documented policies, procedures and business processes in support of the internal control system. In order to ensure compliance, such documentation must include the following:
- Schematic process flows of each function within the payroll operation.
- Written procedures for each step of a business process.
- Record keeping requirements are in regulatory compliance and records are organized and accessible.
- Proper segregation of duties is in place and is enforced.
- Gaps and risks in internal controls have been identified and if not resolved, a plan exists for doing so.

If a third party service provider is used, the control requirements are equally applicable to the processes of the provider. Using such a provider does not absolve an employer from meeting the requirements of SOX.

Company changes

As a key support service for the employees of an organization, changes in policy and structure create corresponding process changes for a payroll organization. A payroll organization that is strongly networked throughout an organization will enhance the opportunity for participation in decision-making and implementation. For example, the implementation of an information system requires the involvement of the payroll organization to ensure proper business process design for payroll, human resources, general ledger and accounts payable integration.

State requirement for employees paid by check

Most states generally require that an employee who receives a paycheck be able to:
- Exchange an employer-provided paycheck for the face value of cash at a financial institution without service charge or discounting.
- Exchange an employer-provided paycheck at a financial institution that is at least located in the same state as the employee and often at a convenient location for the employee.

Direct deposit

The Electronic Funds Transfer Act governs the process of administering direct deposit of employee payroll. The Act prohibits an employer from requiring as a condition of employment, the acceptance of direct deposit by an employee at a *specific financial institution* designated by the employer. The employer may, however, require the employee to accept direct deposit if the employee is allowed to choose the receiving financial institution. The employer may also offer direct deposit as a voluntary alternative to a payment of check or cash.

NACHA
NACHA (formerly an acronym for The National Automated Clearinghouse Association) is a nonprofit organization that acts as the self-regulatory body for the automated clearinghouse (ACH) process of electronic payments. In conjunction with its members, NACHA is responsible for the development, administration and governance of the ACH network which facilitates electronic payments such as the direct deposit of payroll earnings.

Automated Clearinghouse (ACH) process
The primary components or nodes of the system that facilitates direct deposits are the following:
- Employer – initiates the electronic file containing the payment information.
- Originating Financial Institution – receives the file from the employer and initiates processing through the ACH network.
- ACH Network – settles the transactions between the financial institutions.

- Receiving Financial Institution – designated by the employee, receipt of funds is posted to the employee account.
- Employee – designates the receiving financial institution and accesses funds as required.

High level process flow: The high level ACH process flow is per the example below:

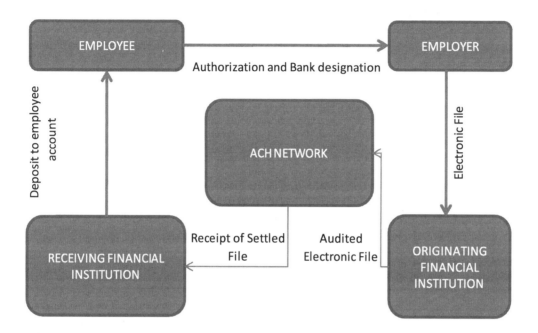

Employee/employer authorization process: The operating rules of the Automated Clearinghouse (ACH) require that direct deposit transactions be preauthorized by the recipient employee. Since a deposit represents a credit to the employee bank account (as opposed to a withdrawal or debit), the rules allow the authorization to be verbal though it is often advised that a signed document also be provided and retained. The employee must provide the following information:
- The name and routing transit number of the receiving financial institution.
- The account number and type of account (i.e. checking or savings) at the receiving financial institution.

Prenotification process: Though not required, a prenotification, often called a prenote, is a zero value transaction that is processed through the ACH system as a test of the validity of the financial institution information provided by the employee. A successful end-to-end processing indicates that a subsequent direct deposit transaction will post appropriately. A prenote failure indicates that the data provided must be corrected prior to initiating a direct deposit. ACH rules require that, if a prenotification is used, it must be processed no later than six banking days before the transmission of an actual direct deposit.

Error correction rules: ACH rules allow for the correction of common errors using what is called a single entry reversal without a documented debit authorization from the employee. Such common errors include incorrect employee, incorrect amount of payment or duplicated payment. The correction must be processed within five days of the original direct deposit transaction. Once the correction entry is successfully cleared by the ACH network, the rules require that the employee must be notified of the correction no later than the same day that the entry was posted to the employee's account.

<u>Routing transit numbers</u>
A routing transfer number is a nine-digit number assigned to a financial institution by a registrar acting on behalf of the American Bankers Association (ABA). The purpose of the number is to assign a unique identifier to a financial institution enabling the proper routing and clearing of transactions. For a direct deposit, the routing number is critical to ensure that the payment is directed to the specific financial institution designated by the employee.

Electronic paycards

A paycard is similar to a credit or debit card in that it contains employee information embedded in a magnetic strip on one side of the card. However, the function of the card is more similar to a gift card in that it allows access to a predetermined amount of cash (i.e. a stored value) by the employee at a financial institution or as a point-of-sale (POS) transaction. The amount of cash authorized by the card (i.e. "preloaded" on the card) is equivalent to the employee net pay. A paycard is intended for employees who do not have access to a banking relationship (so-called *unbanked* or *underbanked* employees) in order to receive direct deposit payments.

<u>Regulation E</u>
Regulation E specifies the implementation rules for the Electronic Fund Transfer Act and was amended to expand the definition of "account" as in bank account, to include a payroll card account. Therefore, paycards are subject to the same regulatory requirements as a direct deposit. In addition, specifies that paycards are subject to the same compulsory use requirements as direct deposits.

Payment reissue

Unclaimed wages are considered to be a form of abandoned property, the owner of which is the employee. Therefore, payments which are not settled to the employee (such as cashing a check, depositing an electronic transfer or withdrawing funds from a paycard), must be reissued to the employee upon request. It is typically a two-step process involving the cancellation of the original transaction (check stop payment, direct deposit reversal or paycard reversal) followed by a subsequent new issue of the payment. If a substantial period of time has elapsed since the original issue, the escheatment laws of the applicable state may impact the ability to reissue. Such laws vary by state but payroll payments are deemed to be abandoned property if unclaimed for a period of years. Unclaimed property is transferred to the state at that time, so claiming the funds becomes an issue between the employee and the state.

Impact of federal banking holidays on employee payments

Federal banking holidays are those in which the Federal Reserve System is closed, preventing the processing of all banking transactions. Therefore, electronic payments which would otherwise be processed on that day must be rescheduled to a day either before or after the holiday. Federal holidays can also impact the deposit of payroll taxes since such deposits cannot be received.

Constructive receipt and payment

The principal of constructive receipt and payment governs the timing of tax withholdings from a payroll disbursement. Employers are required to withhold at the point in time in which an employee is *actually or constructively paid,* which is defined as whenever the payment has been made available to the employee without *substantial limitation or restriction.* The critical nuance in this definition is that the employee need not physically be in possession of funds but simply must have the ability to access the funds (i.e. the funds are available and accessible). The date of withholding corresponds to the date of availability and accessibility.

Governance process regarding frequency and method of payment

Since neither the Fair Labor Standards Act (FLSA) nor the Internal Revenue Code (IRC) address the frequency and method of payment to employees, the process is left to regulation by each of the states. Most states have established a minimum frequency for when employees must be paid while three, Alabama, Florida and Montana are silent on the issue. The frequency varies from weekly (Connecticut, Massachusetts, New Hampshire, Rhode Island and Vermont) to monthly (Alaska, Colorado, Delaware, Idaho, Kansas, Minnesota, North Dakota, South Dakota, Virginia and Wisconsin). Where the method of payment is cash or check, all of the states (and the District of Columbia) either allow the process by regulation or have no specific rule. For direct deposits and paycards, the process is regulated by the Electronic Funds Transfer Act which is further interpreted by Federal Reserve Board Regulation E. The general rule for electronic methods of payment is that the employer can only require participation if the employee is allowed to designate the receiving financial institution.

Importance of communication and confidence in payroll operations

Communication and confidence represent two of the key attributes of quality customer service in not only payroll but any operation. However, the issues of the customers of a payroll operation are most often quite personal; such is the nature of financial information. Therefore, it is imperative that the payroll employees are effectively and comprehensibly trained in order to convey a sense of knowledge and confidence with which to gain the trust of their customers. A competent payroll employee is not necessarily one who knows all of the answers. Rather, competence is a function of familiarity with the many reference sources with which to find the necessary information.

Payroll operation customers and importance of responsiveness

A payroll operation typically services two groups of customers: the employees who rely on the payroll service for accurate payments, and the employer as represented by the management team, from whom regulatory compliance and management reporting are key expectations. As such, responsiveness is a critical attribute for the following reasons:
- Each employee expects to receive an accurate payment on-time.
- Where discrepancies occur, particularly those in which wages are involved, a quick, accurate and reliable resolution is expected.

- Full regulatory compliance is required by the employer, the lack of which can give rise to penalties and legal actions.
- A proper accounting of the periodic transactions created by the payroll process is key to not only financial reporting in compliance with accounting and securities regulation, but to timely and accurate management reporting.

Principles of customer service

The key principles with which to provide effective customer service in a payroll operation are as follows:
- Reliability – accurate, dependable and reliable payments and information, consistently provided.
- Responsiveness – an organizational structure that anticipates the service needs of its customers.
- Assurance – a fully trained and competent staff that is confident in its abilities and able to project the same to its customers.
- Empathy – a recognition that the service needs of its customers are personal and time-sensitive requiring confidence and timely response.
- Tangibles – the equipment, resources and technology with which to facilitate reliability, responsiveness, assurance and empathy.

Resources used to resolve customer payment and withholding issues

Issues involving payment issues such as frequency, method of payment and specific situations such as employee termination are subject to state regulation. An important resource for state laws and regulations is provided by the American Payroll Association (APA) and entitled Guide to State Payroll Laws. Federal tax resources are provided by the Internal Revenue Service and include the following:
- Internal Revenue Code and Regulations
- Revenue Rulings, Revenue Procedures and Publications
- Internal Revenue Bulletins

Federal statutory activity can be monitored via the following:
- Congressional Record
- Federal Register
- SSA/IRS Reporter (Social Security Administration, Internal Revenue Service)

In addition, the IRS offers a tax practitioner section of its website that contains information and links on most subjects of interest to payroll professionals

Compliance/Research and Resources

Escheat law compliance

Escheat laws refer to unclaimed property obligations. Companies who issue checks-for wages, payroll, employee commissions, returnable garnishments, deferred compensation, payroll services or bonuses have a potential (and probable) unclaimed property obligation. States are stepping up their audit focus on unclaimed property as a way to boost their revenue, so the risk of a business being audited for such property will only increase. Business must understand escheat laws that apply to them and comply in all respects. Penalties for failure to file unclaimed property reports vary between states, but typically involve civil penalties and criminal fines and imprisonment.

Verification of amounts remitted to a state as escheat

If all possible property subject to escheat law has been reviewed, the next step is to review the required abandonment period for your state and follow your state's escheat or "unclaimed property" filing rules. Similar to most state tax laws, escheat laws have designated forms and filing dates. Most states have an annual November 1 deadline for filing and remitting unclaimed property. Business owners must reconcile amounts reported as unclaimed property to the source documents that relate to these amounts.

403(b) plans and 457 plans.

Both 403(b) and 457 plans are defined contribution retirement plans; that is, they are retirement savings plans to which employees may contribute with pre-tax dollars.

457 plans are subject to contribution limits that may fluctuate year to year due to inflation. The contribution limits are usually in line with plan 401(k) limits (i.e. higher) than traditional IRA limits. However, unlike 401(k) plans, 457 plans are not subject to early withdrawals penalties. As an additional benefit, contributions to a 457 plan do not count against contribution limits to other types of defined contribution plans. 457 plans are generally available to state and local government employees, and in some cases, non-profit organizations.

403(b) plans are generally available to government employees, and employees of tax-exempt organizations (i.e. schools, churches, etc.). Contribution limits to 403(b) plans are generally in line with those of 401(k) plans. Like 401(k) plans, and unlike 457 plans, 403(b) plans are subject to a 10% tax penalty if money is withdrawn from them before the plan owner reaches age 59 ½.

Accountable and non-accountable employee plans

The terms accountable plans and non-accountable plans refer to employee expense reimbursement methods allowed by the Internal Revenue Service. Under accountable plans, expenses reimbursed to the employee are not considered taxable income to the employee. Rather they are legitimate business expenses incurred in the operation of daily business activities. Non-accountable plans, however, are reimbursement plans that result in taxable income to the employee that receives the reimbursement. Accountable plans and non-accountable plans are not mutually exclusive, and employers can use a mix of the two to accomplish their objectives.

For a reimbursement plan to be considered accountable, it must meet several conditions: expenses must have a business condition, the employee should substantiate the expense with proof of expenditure, and the reimbursement recipient should return any payment in excess of expenses incurred in a timely manner. For these purposes, a timely manner is at least quarterly. Best practices suggest more frequently.

Personal use of company-provided automobiles

Personal use of a company-provided vehicle is any use of the vehicle for non-business purposes. The IRS normally considers such use to be a taxable noncash fringe benefit. An arms-length transaction standard is imposed, and the amount of the benefit is based on several factors including the length of time the vehicle is available to the employee, the specific vehicle or type of vehicle used, and the geographic area of the use. A cents-per-mile calculation is generally not available to establish the value of the benefit unless the taxpayer can prove that the vehicle could have been leased on this basis from a third party.

Dependent care assistance programs

Under the Internal Revenue Code, an employer may provide an employee with up to $5,000 each year in child and dependent care benefits tax-free (no FIT, FUTA, or FICA), if these benefits are provided pursuant to a written, qualified plan called a dependent care assistance program, or DCAP. In most states, such benefits are not subject to state income taxes either. If child and dependent care benefits are provided to an employee outside a DCAP, the benefits are considered taxable income to the employee, and both the employee and the employer must pay taxes on them.

Employee tax benefits
Employees can benefit from the company-sponsored dependent benefit plans in more ways than one. In addition to the dependent care aspect, there also can be tax savings. For instance, assume Fred is in the 25% income tax bracket for 2016 and deposits $5,000 in a dependent care account. His potential income tax savings are $1,250. Fred also saves $383 in payroll taxes; his cumulative tax savings are therefore $1,633. Fred's employer also benefits from a reduction in matching payroll taxes.

Form 668-D

In the event that an individual fails to pay the entirety of his or her taxes due, the Internal Revenue Service may place a levy against the wages of that individual. This is accomplished by an official of the Internal Revenue Service (IRS) serving the individual with a Form 668-A (Notice of Levy) or 668-W (Notice of Levy on Wages, [hence the letter W], Salary, and Other Income). Form 668-A is only effective on a singular basis, whereas Form 668-W is attached to the employee's wages.

For an employee to remove an IRS levy that has been attached by Forms 668-A or 668-W, he or she must satisfy the IRS judgment against him or her. After the judgment has been satisfied, the IRS can release the levy by executing Form 668-D for the employee. Form 668-

- 37 -

D can be executed to release levies against either property or wages. The information contained on Form 668-D contains the taxpayer's personal information, the nature of the levy placed, and the fact that the levy is being released.

Form 668-W

Form 668-W is the form that the Internal Revenue Service files to inform a taxpayer that his or her wages are being garnished or levied due to lack of payment of taxes owed. It is also known as the Notice of Levy on Wages, Salary, and Other Income. Internal Revenue Service (IRS) Form 668-W also assists the taxpayer (whose wages are being garnished) in determining the amount of income that is exempt from the levy. However, if the taxpayer does not fill out the form and return it within three days, the IRS will assume a status of married filing separately with one exemption. IRS Form 668-W supercedes IRS Form W-4 in the calculation of taxes withheld from an employee's payroll whose wages are being garnished. For a taxpayer to have Form 668-W cancelled along with the garnishment of his or her wages, the taxpayer must satisfy his or her tax obligations and obtain IRS Form 668-D, the wage levy release IRS form.

Qualified Medical Child Support Orders (QMCSOs)

Qualified medical child support orders were established as an amendment to the Employee Retirement Income Security Act, or ERISA. In the amendment, ERISA requires that health insurance coverage provided by employers be extended from the covered parent who has been divorced, separated, or not married, to his or her children, if so ordered by state authorities. For a medical child support order to be considered "qualified," it must contain the name and address of the participant and alternate recipient (the alternate recipient may be a state or local official) and it must contain information pertaining to the type of health coverage that must be provided to the child or children named in the qualified medical child support order (QMCSO). QMCSOs may only require that the children be covered under existing plan provisions in all cases except certain administrative capacities. Such capacities are enrollment periods, dependency status, residency status, locality, parents' marital status at time of the child's birth, compliance with court orders, and the allowance of the non-insured parent to file a claim on the insurance of the insured parent on behalf of the child.

Notices that a payroll professional might receive from government agencies

There are many different types of notices that a payroll department may receive from a government agency with which they are legally bound to comply. Such notices may come from federal, state, or local government agencies, depending upon the reason the notice has been sent. Among the most common are wage garnishments for taxes due, and wage garnishment for child support due. Garnishment for taxes due is an example of a federal agency (Internal Revenue Service) notice, while child support garnishments are typically issued by state or local governmental agencies. Other notices received are more administrative in nature, such as notices related to the execution of information laws, such as the USA PATRIOT Act. An example of this type of notice occurs when the payroll office does not have complete personal information (or has complete incorrect personal information) for an employee (such as a missing or incorrect Social Security Number).

Foreign earned income exclusions

The foreign income earned exclusion is the ability of a United States taxpayer to exclude some or all of his or her income earned in a foreign country from taxation in the US. While this income may be excluded for taxation purposes, it must be reported on the taxpayer's annual income tax return. This reporting of foreign income and requesting of exclusion from taxable income is reported on IRS Form 2555, and IRS Form 2555-EZ. In addition to excluding the foreign income, certain housing costs associated with earning foreign income may be used as write offs. Once Form 2555 has been filed, the exclusion remains in effect until the taxpayer revokes the exclusion. To determine eligibility to take the exclusion, one must pass the bona fide residence test (residency of the taxpayer for the entire tax year), physical presence test (present in the country for 330 days), and the tax home test (location of residence). If the taxpayer passes the appropriate tests, he or she may exclude up to $101,300 (for an individual as of 2016) of his or her income earned in a foreign country.

U.S. expatriate taxation

Expatriates of the United States are still required to file income tax returns with the Internal Revenue Service, or IRS. As long as taxpayers pass the bona fide residency tests, they are often allowed to exclude income earned in their country of residence from taxation in the United States, up to $101,300 for an individual as of 2016. Additionally, the taxpayer may be allowed to deduct housing expenses associated with the foreign income earned.

If the United States and the country in which the expatriate resides have tax treaties in place, taxpayers may file for credits that will generally cover their taxes due. This helps prevent the double taxation of income earned, but the taxpayer must file an income tax return in his or her country to receive these credits. Expatriates may also be subject to income taxation in the states in which they resided before their expatriation. According to states' laws, the taxpayer's tax domicile may still be the state in which they used to live if they meet any of a number of tests (voting district, driver's license registration, etc.)

Visa status and taxation

Depending upon the residency and visa status of an individual in the United States, they may or may not have to report income and pay income taxes in the US. Unlike green card holders, legal residents in the US on non-immigrant visas may not have to report their income and pay taxes on that income. Non-immigrant visa holders will become residents after 183 days in the US, and will likely have to report income if they are in the US any longer than that. The 183 day rule is cumulative for three years and assigns a weighting of one-third of a day for each day in residence the prior year, and one-sixth for each day in residence in the year before that. One day in the current year, three days in the prior year, and six days in the year before would equal three days of residency in the current year for the weighted rule. In the event that a non-immigrant worker pays income tax and is in the US for fewer than 183 weighted days, they may be entitled to receive that money back from the government.

Student exemption for FICA

FICA taxes, or Federal Insurance Contribution Act, refer to taxes collected from employees' payrolls to help fund Social Security and Medicare. According to the Internal Revenue

Service's (IRS) Treasury Decision 9167 (published in December of 2004), some students with earned income may be exempt from paying FICA taxes. For a student to receive the exemption from FICA taxes, they must be employed at a school, college, or university where they are engaged in a course of study. The employer determines whether or not the employee's main relationship with the institution is education or employment, subject to IRS audit. For the employee to receive the exemption, the employer must determine that the employee's main relationship with the institution is that of a student. IRS Safe Harbor rules help define students as at least half-time undergraduate or half-time graduate students who are not full-time employees and are not eligible for certain job-related benefits from the institution. Additionally, graduate students who are graduating in the current semester but are not at least half-time students also qualify for the exemption.

Public sector exemption for FICA

When Social Security was established in 1935, states governments were allowed to opt-in or opt-out of the Social Security retirement program. While many states opted-in to the program over time, ten states (as of 2016) have not opted-in, and the employees of the governments of the states are exempt from paying FICA taxes. The states are Texas, Louisiana, Colorado, Alaska, California, Massachusetts, Nevada, Ohio, Illinois, and Maine. Employees of the governments of these states are exempt from paying into the Social Security and Medicare systems, but this also precludes them from receiving Social Security and Medicare benefits. In addition to certain states' employees being exempt from FICA taxes, many federal employees and contractors are also exempt from paying into the Social Security and Medicare systems.

HIPAA (Health Insurance Portability and Accountability Act) payroll regulations

The Health Insurance Portability and Accountability Act of 1996, or HIPAA, addresses far reaching privacy issues. In due course, payroll departments are especially affected by the HIPAA legislation, because so much of the information that they administer is of a personal and sensitive nature. Payroll professionals are privy to certain information that employees may not want made public, such as a reason for being away from the job (which may include medical reasons). Payroll professionals are entitled, however, to HIPAA sensitive information since they are instrumental in setting up health care coverage for individuals and they provide other services that make this information needful. Since payroll professionals have access to such personal information, including health and wellness information, it is imperative that they observe HIPAA rules regarding the privacy of each employee and not share it with departments that are not cleared for HIPAA information.

Form W-4P

Internal Revenue Service (IRS) Form W-4P (also known as the Withholding Certificate for Pension or Annuity Payments) functions similarly to the parent IRS Form W-4, in that it assists taxpayers in determining the withholding amounts for taxes to be paid on income received. IRS Form W-4P is specifically filed for taxes to be withheld from pensions, annuities, and other forms of deferred compensation (hence the P addendum on the end of the form name). It is important for individuals who receive payments from the above-mentioned types of compensation to file IRS Form W-4P to ensure that the appropriate amount of withholding is being taken from payments sent. If this form is not filed with the payer, the default withholding for these types of payments assumes married-filing-jointly with three exemptions. Form W-4P must only be filed once, and the payer will continue to withhold based on the assumptions of the original Form W-4P until the payee files a new Form W-4P.

Form 8233

Internal Revenue Service (IRS) Form 8233 is the Exemption from Withholding on Compensation for Independent (and Certain Dependent) Personal Services of a Non-Resident Alien Individual form. Non-resident aliens who wish to claim an exemption from federal tax withholding on their payroll may file IRS Form 8233. Form 8233 will generally allow an exemption of withholding from payroll if the non-resident alien's country of citizenship has a tax treaty with the United States that requires or allows such an exemption. IRS Form 8233 assists the taxpayer in determining whether or not he or she qualifies for the exemption, and collects all pertinent information to provide to the Internal Revenue Service. When filing IRS Form 8233, the taxpayer must submit a statement detailing why and under what tax treaty he or she are eligible to receive the payroll withholding exemption.

Allocated tips

The term *allocated tips* refers to an amount of tip money that is assigned to an individual by his or her employer. Allocated tips are reported in addition to tips that are reported as received by the employee. For an employer to allocate tips, the employer must be in a business (such as a restaurant) that is required to allocate tips to its employees, the employee must have reported tips for less than eight percent of food and drink sales that he or she served, and the employee must not be a participant in an attributed tip income program. Payroll departments must report allocated tips on IRS Form W-2 (box 8) to the tipped employee. When the employee files his or her income tax return, the employee must file IRS Form 4137 which reports allocated tips as income received. Employers reporting allocated tips on behalf of tipped employees generally do so to assist the employee in determining the amount of withholding for which he or she should file IRS Form W-4.

COBRA

Congress passed the landmark Consolidated Omnibus Budget Reconciliation Act (COBRA) health benefit provisions in 1986. The law amends the Employee Retirement Income Security Act, the Internal Revenue Code and the Public Health Service Act to provide continuation of group health coverage that otherwise might be terminated. COBRA provides certain former employees, retirees, spouses, former spouses, and dependent children the right to temporary continuation of health coverage at group rates. This coverage, however, is only available when coverage is lost due to certain specific events. Group health coverage for COBRA participants is usually more expensive than health coverage for active employees, since usually the employer pays a part of the premium for active employees while COBRA participants generally pay the entire premium themselves. It is ordinarily less expensive, though, than individual health coverage.

Process
Employers must notify plan administrators of a qualifying event within 30 days after an employee's death, termination, reduced hours of employment or entitlement to Medicare. A qualified beneficiary must notify the plan administrator of a qualifying event within 60 days

after divorce or legal separation or a child's ceasing to be covered as a dependent under plan rules. Plan participants and beneficiaries generally must be sent an election notice not later than 14 days after the plan administrator receives notice that a qualifying event has occurred. The individual then has 60 days to decide whether to elect COBRA continuation coverage. The person has 45 days after electing coverage to pay the initial premium.

Required elements
There are three elements to qualifying for COBRA benefits. COBRA establishes specific criteria for plans, qualified beneficiaries, and qualifying events: 1) Plan coverage. Group health plans for employers with 20 or more employees on more than 50 percent of its typical business days in the previous calendar year are subject to COBRA. Both full and part-time employees are counted to determine whether a plan is subject to COBRA. 2) Qualified beneficiaries. A qualified beneficiary generally is an individual covered by a group health plan on the day before a qualifying event who is an employee, the employee's spouse, or an employee's dependent child. 3) Qualifying events. Qualifying events are certain events that would cause an individual to lose health coverage. The type of qualifying event will determine who the qualified beneficiaries are and the amount of time that a plan must offer the health coverage to them under COBRA.

Qualification for extended periods of COBRA continuation coverage
Disability can extend the 18-month period of continuation coverage for a qualifying event that is a termination of employment or reduction of hours. To qualify for additional months of COBRA continuation coverage, the qualified beneficiary must: 1) have a ruling from the Social Security Administration that he or she became disabled within the first 60 days of COBRA continuation coverage; and 2) send the plan a copy of the Social Security ruling letter within 60 days of receipt, but prior to expiration of the 18-month period of coverage. If these requirements are met, the entire family qualifies for an additional 11 months of COBRA continuation coverage. Plans can charge 150% of the premium cost for the extended period of coverage.

Guidelines to file and appeal claims for benefits
Health plan rules must explain how to obtain benefits and must include written procedures for processing claims. Claims procedures must be described in the Summary Plan Description. Employees should submit a claim for benefits in accordance with the plan's rules for filing claims. If the claim is denied, he or she must be given notice of the denial in writing generally within 90 days after the claim is filed. The notice should state the reasons for the denial, any additional information needed to support the claim, and procedures for appealing the denial. The employee will have at least 60 days to appeal a denial and must receive a decision on the appeal generally within 60 days after that.

Covered benefits
Qualified beneficiaries must be offered coverage identical to that available to similarly situated beneficiaries who are not receiving COBRA coverage under the plan (generally, the same coverage that the qualified beneficiary had immediately before qualifying for continuation coverage). A change in the benefits under the plan for the active employees will also apply to qualified beneficiaries. Qualified beneficiaries must be allowed to make the same choices given to non-COBRA beneficiaries under the plan, such as during periods of open enrollment by the plan. COBRA coverage begins on the date that health care coverage would otherwise have been lost by reason of a qualifying event and will stop at the end of the maximum period.

Coverage for divorced spouses of employees

Under COBRA, participants, covered spouses and dependent children may continue their plan coverage for a limited time when they would otherwise lose coverage due to a particular event, such as divorce (or legal separation). A covered employee's spouse who would lose coverage due to a divorce may elect to continue coverage under the plan for a maximum time of 36 months. A qualified beneficiary must notify the plan administrator of a qualifying event within 60 days after divorce or a legal separation. After being notified of a divorce, the plan administrator must give notice, generally within 14 days, to the qualified beneficiary of the right to elect COBRA continuation coverage.

Who pays for COBRA coverage

Beneficiaries may be required to pay for COBRA coverage. The premium cannot exceed 102% of the cost to the plan for similarly situated individuals who have not incurred a qualifying event, including both the portion paid by employees and any portion paid by the employer before the qualifying event, plus 2 percent for administrative costs. For qualified beneficiaries receiving the 11 month disability extension of coverage, the premium for those additional months may be increased to 150 percent of the plan's total cost of coverage. COBRA premiums may be increased if the costs to the plan increase but generally must be fixed in advance of each 12-month premium cycle. The plan must allow you to pay premiums on a monthly basis if you ask to do so, and the plan may allow you to make payments at other intervals (weekly or quarterly).

Period of coverage

COBRA establishes required periods of coverage for continuation health benefits. A plan, however, may provide longer periods of coverage beyond those required by COBRA. COBRA beneficiaries generally are eligible for group coverage during a maximum of 18 months for qualifying events due to employment termination or reduction of hours of work. Certain qualifying events, or a second qualifying event during the initial period of coverage, may permit a beneficiary to receive a maximum of 36 months of coverage. It may end earlier for reasons such as but not limited to the premiums not being paid in a timely manner; the employer ceasing to maintain any group health plan; or after the COBRA election, a beneficiary becomes entitled to Medicare benefits.

FMLA

The Family and Medical Leave Act (FMLA), effective Aug. 5, 1993, requires an employer to maintain coverage under any group health plan for an employee on FMLA leave under the same conditions the coverage would have been provided if the employee had continued working. Coverage provided under the FMLA is not COBRA coverage, and FMLA leave is not a qualifying event under COBRA. A COBRA qualifying event may occur, however, when an employer's obligation to maintain health benefits under FMLA ceases, such as when an employee notifies an employer of his or her intent not to return to work. COBRA continuation coverage laws are administered by several agencies. The Departments of Labor and Treasury have jurisdiction over private-sector health group health plans. The Department of Health and Human Services administers the continuation coverage law as it affects public-sector health plans.

Amount employees must pay for coverage

Employers may pay all or part of workers' group health premiums. Under COBRA, as a former employee no longer receiving benefits, the employee will usually pay the entire premium amount, that is, the portion of the premium that was paid as an active employee and the amount of the contribution made by the employer. In addition, there may be a 2% administrative fee. While COBRA rates may seem high, the former employee will be paying group premium rates, which are usually lower than individual rates. Since it is likely that there will be a lapse of a month or more between the date of layoff and the time an employee makes the COBRA election decision, the employee may have to pay health premiums retroactively-from the time of separation from the company. The first premium, for instance, will cover the entire time since the last day of employment.

Calculating an employee's share of short-term disability

Dana Reagan chose to pay for half of her 40 percent share of the short-term disability insurance via her corporate cafeteria plan. As a result, total payments are composed of the following: 20 percent pre-tax employee contribution; 20 percent after tax employee contribution; and 60 percent employer contribution. Under such an arrangement, 80 percent of the weekly short-term disability payments are subject to income taxes (the employer contribution plus her pre-tax contribution). Assuming Dana's weekly policy benefit is $350, her taxable income increase is $280 (80% x $350). With a third-party liability insurance plan, the employee may ask the insurance carrier to be responsible for all withholding by filing a Form W-4S. If this responsibility is transferred by the insurance carrier to the employer, the company must report on Form W-2 the amount of taxable income that was received by an employee.

FMLA

The federal Family and Medical Leave Act (FMLA) became effective on Aug. 5, 1993, for most employers. If a collective bargaining agreement (CBA) was in effect on that date, FMLA became effective on the expiration date of the CBA or Feb. 5, 1994, whichever was earlier. All private, state, local and most federal employees are covered by the act. FMLA entitles eligible employees to take up to 12 weeks of unpaid, job-protected leave in a 12-month period for specified family and medical reasons. The employer may elect to use the calendar year, a fixed 12-month period or fiscal year, or a 12-month period prior to or after the commencement of leave as the 12-month period. The law contains provisions on employer coverage; employee eligibility for the law's benefits; entitlement to leave, maintenance of health benefits during leave, and job restoration after leave; among other provisions.

The Family & Medical Leave Act (FMLA) allows eligible employees to take up to 12 weeks of unpaid leave for certain family events, including childbirth, adoption to care for a parent or spouse with a serious medical condition, or if the employee has a serious medical condition. Here is an illustration of the FMLA being applied: Sarah will go on maternity leave soon. She has 15 days of sick leave and vacation pay remaining. Short-term disability insurance covers 67 percent of her salary (two-thirds) beginning in the fourth week, and continuing through the 10th week of her leave. Under FMLA provisions, Sarah is entitled to 12 weeks of unpaid leave. In this case, Sarah's company plan allows her to receive her entire salary for 15 days (her remaining paid leave), and two-thirds of her salary through the 10th week of her leave. The remaining two weeks covered by the FMLA would be without pay.

Eligibility requirements and reasons to take the leave
For Family and Medical Leave Act benefits, an employee must: 1) work for a covered employer, 2) have worked for the employer for 12 months, 3) have worked at least 1,250

hours over those 12 months, and 4) Work at a location in the U.S or U.S. possession where at least 50 employees are employed by the employer within 75 miles. A covered employer must grant an eligible employee up to a total of 12 workweeks of unpaid leave during any 12-month period for any of the following reasons:

- For the birth and care of the newborn child of the employee;
- For placement with the employee of a son or daughter for adoption or foster care;
- To care for an immediate family member (spouse, child, or parent) with a serious health condition; or
- To take medical leave when the employee is unable to work because of a serious health condition.
- For qualifying exigencies related to certain National Guard or Reserves contingency operations and active duty status.

Calculation of time off and paid leave provisions
The 12-month period of time off for the Family & Medical Leave Act can be calculated by employers using one of four options: 1) the calendar year; 2) any fixed 12-month "leave year" such as a fiscal year, a year required by state law, or a year starting on the employee's "anniversary" date; 3) the 12-month period measured forward from the date any employee's first FMLA leave begins; or 4) a "rolling" 12-month period measured backward from the date an employee uses FMLA leave. The FMLA only requires unpaid leave, and the law allows an employee to elect, or the employer to require the employee, to use accrued paid leave for some or all of the FMLA leave period.

Inquiries that can be made by an employer
An employer can only make inquiries about the employee on his or her leave of absence to the employee. The employer may ask the employee questions in order to confirm whether the leave or leave request under review qualifies for FMLA purposes, and may require periodic status reports and confirmation of the employee's intent to return to work after leave. The employer may also require the employee to obtain additional medical certification at the employer's expense, or recertification while on FMLA leave. The employer may also have their health care provider representative contact the employee's health care provider, with employee consent, to clarify information in the medical certification or to confirm that it was provided by the health care provider. In this inquiry, the employer may not seek additional information regarding the employee's health condition or that of a family member.

Totalization agreements

The United States has entered into agreements, called totalization agreements, with several nations for the purpose of avoiding double taxation of income with respect to social security taxes. These agreements must be taken into account when determining whether any alien is subject to the United States Social Security/Medicare tax, or whether any U.S. citizen or resident alien is subject to the social security taxes of a foreign country. The following nations have entered into Totalization Agreements with the United States: Australia, Austria, Belgium, Canada, Chile, Czech Republic, Denmark, Finland, France, Germany, Greece, Ireland, Italy, Japan, Luxembourg, Netherlands, Norway, Poland, Portugal, South Korea, Spain, Sweden, Switzerland, and United Kingdom.

Requirements for U.S. citizens and resident aliens abroad who file tax returns

If employees are citizens of the United States or are resident aliens living or traveling outside the United States, they generally are required to file their income tax returns, estate tax returns, and gift tax returns and pay estimated tax in the same way as those residing in the United States. An employee's income, filing status, and age generally determine whether you must file a return. Generally, the employee must file a return if their gross income from worldwide sources is at least the amount shown for your filing status in the Filing Requirements table in Chapter 1 of Publication 54, Tax Guide for U.S. Citizens and Resident Aliens Abroad.

Withholding employee deductions for charitable contributions

Many employers encourage employees to give charitable contributions such as the United Way. The employers will have employees sign a pledge card that authorizes certain amounts to be deducted from the employee's paycheck. A lump-sum payment of employee contributions and any matching amounts by employers are sent to the charity. The IRS requires donors to have written proof from a charity if the amount of a contribution exceeds $250. But, this requirement is for individual contributions of $250 or more, and it is unlikely that a single payroll deduction (each of which is considered an individual contribution) will exceed this limit. Furthermore, charities are unlikely to have enough information to provide written substantiation because contributions are received as a lump-sum payment from the employer. The IRS allows employees to use their year-end paycheck advice as part of the documentation needed to meet proof of contribution requirements.

Wage garnishment

Restrictions
The amount of pay subject to garnishment is based on an employee's "disposable earnings," which is the amount left after legally required deductions are made. Examples of such deductions include federal, state, and local taxes, the employee's share of State Unemployment Insurance and Social Security. It also includes withholdings for employee retirement systems required by law. Deductions not required by law - such as those for voluntary wage assignments, union dues, health and life insurance, contributions to charitable causes, purchases of savings bonds, retirement plan contributions (except those required by law) and payments to employers for payroll advances or purchases of merchandise - usually may not be subtracted from gross earnings when calculating disposable earnings under the Consumer Credit Protection Act.

Restrictions on wage garnishment for child support and alimony
Specific restrictions apply to court orders for child support or alimony. The garnishment law allows up to 50 percent of a worker's disposable earnings to be garnished for these purposes if the worker is supporting another spouse or child, or up to 60 percent if the worker is not. An additional 5 percent may be garnished for support payments more than 12 weeks in arrears. The wage garnishment law specifies that the garnishment restrictions do not apply to certain bankruptcy court orders, or to debts due for federal or state taxes. If a state wage garnishment law differs from the Consumer Credit Protection Act, the law resulting in the smaller garnishment must be observed.

Maximum amounts garnished during pay periods

The law sets the maximum amount that may be garnished in any workweek or pay period, regardless of the number of garnishment orders received by the employer. For ordinary garnishments (i.e., those not for support, bankruptcy, or any state or federal tax), the weekly amount may not exceed the lesser of: 25% of the employee's disposable earnings, or the amount by which an employee's disposable earnings are greater than 30 times the federal minimum wage (currently in 2016, $7.25 an hour). For instance, if the pay period is weekly and disposable earnings are $217.50 ($7.25 x 30) or less, there can be no garnishment. A maximum of 25% can be garnished, if disposable income earnings are $290 or more. When pay periods cover more than one week, multiples of the weekly restrictions must be used to calculate the maximum amounts that may be garnished.

Statutory tests for wage garnishment

The following examples illustrate the statutory tests for determining the amounts that are subject to wage garnishment: 1) An employee's gross earnings in a particular week are $263.00. After deductions required by law, the disposable earnings are $233.00. In this week $15.50 may be garnished, since only the amount over $217.50 may be garnished where the disposable earnings are $290.00 or less. The employee would be paid $217.50. 2) An employee's gross earnings in a particular workweek are $402.00. After deductions required by law, the disposable earnings are $368.00. In this week 25% of the disposable earnings may be garnished. ($368.00 x 25% = $92.00). The employee would be paid $276.00.

U.S. Department of Labor wage determinations

Wage determinations made by the U.S. Department of Labor are developed based on available data showing the rates that are prevailing in a specific locality. Where a single rate is paid to a majority (more than 50%) of the workers in a classification of service employees engaged in similar work in a particular locality, that rate is determined to prevail. When information is used from the Bureau of Labor Statistics (BLS) or other surveys, statistical measurements of central tendency (median) and the average (mean) are considered reliable indicators of the prevailing rate. Which of these statistical measurements will be applied in a given case will be determined after a careful analysis of the overall survey, separate classification data, patterns existing between survey periods, and the way separate classification data interrelate. Use of the median is the general rule. However, the mean may be used in certain situations.

New hire reporting program

New hire reporting is the process by which you, as an employer, report information on your newly hired employees to a designated state agency shortly after the date of hire. New hire reports are matched against child support records at the state and national levels to locate parents who owe child support. This is especially helpful for interstate cases (in which one parent lives in a different state from his or her child), which are often the most difficult cases for states to resolve. With new hire reporting, state child support enforcement agencies have the ability to issue income-withholding orders, the most effective means of collecting child support, more quickly.

Wage assignments

The term *wage assignment* refers to the responsibility of the payroll department of an employer to send a portion of an employee's payroll to a third party on the employee's behalf. Wage assignments may or may not be voluntary. Involuntary wage assignments are typically put in place when the employee has been negligent in meeting a responsibility (i.e. loan debtor, child-support), while voluntary wage assignments are typically chosen for convenience or to guarantee against missing payments. Wage assignments are most commonly associated with child support payments, but assignments may also be made to other third parties such as debtors. A common use of wage assignments on an employer's part is to make a loan to an employee and assign part of his or her wages to pay back the loan. This arrangement may only be executed with the consent of the employee. Wage assignments are not especially effective with individuals who are self-employed or work in a cash-only business.

United States Citizenship and Immigration Services (USCIS) requirements

The United States Citizenship and Immigration Services, or USCIS, places certain requirements upon payroll departments of business that employee people who may not yet be citizens of the United States. For non-citizen workers to legally work in the United States, the workers must have one of several of certain statuses, and the payroll department of the employing business must make sure one of these statuses are in existence. The H-1B Visa requires that the worker be employed in a specialty job that requires higher education. The employer must then file Form ETA-9035 and Form I-129 on behalf of the worker. Other than H-1B Visas, a worker may be higher as a temporary worker who does not intend to stay in the United States, or a permanent worker that does plan on staying in the United States. For an employer to hire a permanent worker, that employer must prove that there are not ample US workers to fill the job at the prevailing wage, and that hiring a non-US worker will not harm the work environment or wages received by US workers.

Employee Retirement Income Security Act (ERISA)

The Employee Retirement Income Security Act of 1974, or ERISA, was established to help protect the rights and financial security of retirees who are and were dependent on pensions for their retirement funding. ERISA only applies to private companies that establish pension plans; it does not require that all companies establish them for their employees. ERISA has been extended beyond only defined benefit pension plans to cover all types of qualified defined contribution plans provided by employers. ERISA mostly covers the administrative necessities of the plan, and does not set a minimum dollar amount contribution on behalf of the employer. The administrative guidelines that ERISA established require that the employer give the participant information regarding the plan, define minimum contributions for participation in the plan, establish a reasonable vesting schedule, define the method of benefit accrual and how the plan will be funded, sets up the need for a fiduciary to be responsible for the plan, and allows participants to sue the fiduciary for failing to act in a manner consistent with a fiduciary.

Immigration Reform and Control Act of 1986 (IRCA

The Immigration Reform and Control Act of 1986, commonly referred to with the acronym IRCA, was a law that made it illegal for an employer to hire an illegal alien (with knowledge that the worker was illegally present in the United States). This law affects businesses of greater than three employees, and the payroll department of each business must determine (via reasonable best efforts) whether or not the worker was illegally in the United States. To help payroll professionals determine the eligibility of aliens to be employed in the United States, the IRCA law established Form I-9, or the Employment Eligibility Verification Form. It is incumbent upon the employer (and thus its payroll department) to obtain and verify the information required on Form I-9 for all workers. This form also assists workers who are legally in the United States in providing documentation to prove that they may legally work in the United States.

Tax benefits for adoption

United States citizen taxpayers may qualify for a non-refundable tax credit if they incurred qualified adoption expenses by filing form 8839. For tax year 2016, the maximum credit allowed is $13,460. To receive that maximum credit the taxpayer must have incurred qualified expenses in the adoption of a child. Qualified expenses are defined as "…reasonable and necessary expenses paid in connection with and for the principal purpose of legally adopting an eligible child." The credit begins to phase-out if the taxpayer's modified adjusted gross income exceeds $201,920, and anyone making greater than $241,920 is no longer eligible for the credit. Since the credit is non-refundable, if the credit exceeds the taxpayer's tax bill, the amount remaining may be rolled forward to offset future tax bills for up to five years.

In the event that an employer assisted an employee in the adoption of a child, the employee may exclude the assistance given from his or her earned income, but may not use the amount with which the employer assisted to apply toward the adoption credit.

Employer-provided loans

Employers may make loans to employees as long as the loan agreement is in writing and the employee consents to the loan. Additionally, employees may have the loans deducted from the payroll check before the check is written to them. This is convenient to the employee in that he or she does not have the responsibility of manually paying a loan payment, and the employer benefits from guaranteed receipt of funds. In the event that the employee does not have to pay back a loan made, it could be considered taxable income to the employee. The laws vary state by state; some states will allow loan deductions from payrolls to effectively bring employees below minimum wage, while others may not. Loan payments made are not considered tax deductions, and do not come out of the employee's payroll check on a pre-tax basis.

Form W-2

Filing due dates and extensions
The filing due dates for the six copies of Form W-2 as follows:
- Copy A which is provided to the Social Security Administration (SSA) must be filed *no later than the last day of February for the year ended the previous December*.
- Copies B, C & 2 which is provided to the Employee *no later than the last day of January for the year ended the previous December*.

- Copy D is retained by the employer.
- Copy 1 is provided to the City, State or Local Tax Agency of the employee, filing dates vary by state.

A 30-day extension of time to file copy A with the SSA may be requested prior to the original due date using Form 8809. A request for an extension of time to file copies B, C & 2 with employees may be requested from the Internal Revenue Service (IRS) by letter.

Note that the due date for electronic filing (for the SSA copy) is the first day of April.

Requirement to file electronically
Employers who file no less than 250 Forms W-2 must do so electronically; failure to do so may result in a penalty. Employers who file less than 250 Forms W-2 may voluntarily file electronically. In addition, the IRS offers a service entitled Business Services Online (BSO) is which employers may complete individual on-line Forms W-2 for automatic transfer to the SSA. A waiver from electronic filing may be requested from the Internal Revenue Service (IRS) using form 8508 but must be submitted no later than 45 days before the Form W-2 filing due date.

Payment in January for work done in December
Wages to be reported on Form W-2 for an employee represent the amounts constructively paid during the calendar year. Constructive payment (or from the employee perspective, constructive receipt) is deemed to occur on the date in which the earnings are made available and accessible to the employee. For example, if an employee worked during the period December 1 through December 31 and the employee received access to the funds on January 2, the earnings are to be reported in the new calendar year and not the previous year just ended.

Boxes a-f
The purpose of each of boxes a through f is as follows:
- Box a – the social security number of the employee that corresponds to the employee's social security card. If the employee has applied for but not yet received a card, box a should contain the phrase, "applied for."
- Box b – the Employer Identification Number (EIN); note that it must correspond to the EIN used for employment tax returns. If the employer has applied for but not yet received an EIN, box b should contain the phrase, "applied for."
- Box c – the name, address and zip code of the employer, again corresponding to the employment tax returns.
- Box d – provided for the voluntary use of employers as a control number; not mandatory.
- Box e – the first name, middle initial and last name of the employee.
- Box f – the address and zip code of the employee.

Box 1
Box 1 of Form W-2, *Wage and Tax Statement* exists for the purpose of reporting all taxable wages, tips and other compensation of an employee. The types of income that must be included in Box 1 are as follows:
1. Wages, bonuses, prizes and awards.
2. Noncash payments including certain fringe benefits.

3. Tips reported by the employee to the employer.
4. Certain employee business expense reimbursements.
5. Accident and health insurance premiums for 2% shareholder/employees paid by an S corporation.
6. Taxable benefits from a section 125 cafeteria plan.
7. Employee contributions to an Archer MSA.
8. Employer contributions to an Archer MSA includible as income to the employee.
9. Employer contributions for certain qualified long term care service.
10. Taxable cost of group term life insurance exceeding $50,000 in coverage.
11. Payments for job-related educational expenses or under a nonaccountable plan.
12. Employer payment for employee share of social security and/or Medicare.
13. Designated Roth IRA contributions.
14. Distributions from a Nonqualified Deferred Compensation Plan (NDCP).
15. Amounts includible under section 457(f).
16. Certain statutory employee payments.
17. Certain split-dollar insurance costs.
18. Employee contributions to Health Savings Accounts (HSA).
19. Employer contributions to Health Savings Accounts (HAS).
20. Section 409A amounts for an NQDC plan.
21. All other compensation includible.

Boxes 2, 4 and 6
The purposes of boxes 2, 4 and 6 are as follows:
- Box 2 is for purpose of reporting the amount of federal income taxes withheld from the employee, including any 20% withholding amounts for so-called golden parachute payments.
- Box 4 is for the purpose of reporting the amount of social security tax withheld (including on tip income) from the employee and should not exceed the specified maximum amount of annual tax (for example, the maximum withholding for 2016 is $7,347, or 6.2% of the first $118,500 in earnings).
- Box 6 is for the purpose of reporting the amount of Medicare tax withheld (including on tip income) from the employee.

Box 3
Box 1 wages include all earnings subject to tax without limitation. Box 3 earnings are subject to a ceiling amount beyond which social security tax is not applicable. For the calendar year 2016, the maximum amount of earnings upon which social security tax is applicable was $118,500. Therefore the amount of earnings to report in box 3 is the lesser of box 1 or $118,500.

Box 5
Box 3 wages represent the amount of earnings which are subject to social security taxes. This amount is limited by statute which for 2016 is $118,500. Box 5 wages represent the amount of earnings which are subject to Medicare taxes which are not subject to limitation. Therefore, the amount reported in box 5 is the same as the wages reported in box 1.

Boxes 7 and 8
Box 7 of Form W-2 is intended for reporting the amount of tip income received by an employee and reported to an employer that is subject to social security and Medicare withholding. The amount shown should not exceed the maximum social security wage base

for the year ($118,500 for the year 2016) and should also be included in Box 1 (Wages) and Box 5 (Medicare wages). Box 8 is intended for food and beverage employers who allocate tips to employees. The total amount so allocated is to be entered in this box but is not to be included in Boxes 1, 3, 5 and 7.

<u>Box 10</u>
The dependent care benefits to be included in Box 10 of Form W-2 include the following:
- The fair market value (FMV) of in-kind benefits provided to the employee by the employer.
- Cash amounts paid directly to a third party provider by the employer on behalf of the employee or reimbursements paid directly to the employee.
- Section125 dependent care benefits from pre-tax contributions made by the employee.

<u>Box 11</u>
The information required to be reported in Box 11 of Form W-2 is intended to enable the Social Security Administration (SSA) to ascertain the proper year for correct application of the social security earnings test and correct payment of benefits. The amounts to be included in Box 11 are distributions to an employee from a nongovernmental section 457(b) plan or a nonqualified plan.

<u>Box 12</u>
Box 12 of Form W-2, *Wage and Tax Statement* exists for the purpose of reporting up to four letter codes (in boxes 12a-12d). Four of the 31 possible codes applicable to Box 12 of Form W-2 are as follows:
1. Code A – used for reporting the amount of social security or RRTA tax on tip income that could not be withheld from employees due to a lack of available funds.
2. Code B – used for reporting the amount of Medicare tax on tip income that could not be withheld from employees due to a lack of available funds.
3. Code C – used for reporting the taxable cost of group term life insurance that exceeds $50,000 in coverage amount.
4. Code D – used for reporting the amount of wages deferred to a section 401(k) plan.

<u>Box 13</u>
The three available checkboxes in Box 13 of Form W-2 are as follows:
1. Statutory Employee – used to identify the employee as a so-called statutory employee, defined as a worker who is an independent contractor under the rules of common-law but treated by statute as an employee.
2. Retirement Plan – used to identify the employee as a participant in any of seven types of retirement plans:
   a. A section 401(a) or (k) qualified pension, profit-sharing or stock bonus plan.
   b. A section 403(a) annuity plan.
   c. A section 403(b) custodial account.
   d. A simplified employee plan.
   e. A SIMPLE retirement account.
   f. A 501(c) trust.
   g. A plan for federal, state or local government employees.
3. Third Party Sick Pay – used to identify the employee as the recipient of sick pay provided by a third party.

<u>Box 14</u>
Box 14 of Form W-2 is provided for purpose of reporting any other information which may be useful to the employee. Examples include the following:
- Annual vehicle lease value, if 100% included in income.
- State Disability Insurance (SDI) withholding.
- Union dues.
- Uniform payments.
- Health insurance premiums.
- Educational assistance payments.

<u>Boxes 15-20</u>
The purpose of boxes 15-20 of Form W-2 is to report income and withholding information required by state and local jurisdictions. A total of two jurisdictions can be reported; a separate form is required if additional reporting is required. The specific boxes are as follows:
- Box 15 – used for the two-digit state code and state identification number.
- Box 16 – used to report the amount of wages, salaries and tips taxable in the state jurisdiction.
- Box 17 – used to report the amount of state income tax withheld.
- Box 18 – used to report the amount of wages salaries and tips taxable in the local jurisdiction.
- Box 19 – used to report the amount of local income tax withheld.
- Box 20 – used to report the name of the locality to which the income and withholding is applicable.

Form W-2C

Form W-2C is intended to correct errors on previously filed Forms W-2 or W-2C such as incorrect name, social security number or wage and withholding amounts. Form W-2C should be filed as soon as possible after the detection of Form W-2 errors. The fields which must be completed on the Form W-2C are only those that are to be changed from the original Form W-2 submission. For example, if only the name or social security number is to be changed, then only the appropriate boxes a - i need be used. The remaining fields should be left blank. If there are corrections to wages and/or withholding amounts such that the reconciliation of the Forms W-2 no longer corresponds to the previously filed employment tax returns (such as Form 941), amended returns (Form 941X) may also need be filed.

Form W-3

Form W-3 is filed only when copy A of Form W-2 is filed with the Social Security Administration (SSA) in paper form. Form W-3 is essentially the "cover sheet" for the transmittal of Forms W-2, even if only a single W-2 is to be filed. However, if no less than 250 Forms W-2 are to be filed with the SSA, the filing must be by electronic means rather than paper. Therefore, Form W-3 is not required for electronic filing.

Form W-3C

Form W-3C is required whenever a Form W-2C, copy A is filed in paper form with the Social Security Administration (SSA). However, as with Form W-3, electronic filing (required if no less than 250 Forms W-2 are to be filed) eliminates the necessity of filing Form W-3C.

Form 843

Form 843 must be filed in order to claim a refund or request an abatement of certain taxes, penalties, fees, interest and additional taxes. A separate form must be filed for each combination of tax or fee period and type of tax or fee by either the taxpayer or representative under power of attorney (using Form 2848 Power of Attorney). The form must be filed in either the Internal Revenue Service (IRS) office that corresponds to any notice received or the IRS office at which the corresponding year tax return is filed.

Form 940

Form 940 is required to be filed whenever at least one of the following conditions is met:
- Wages of $1,500 or more were paid to at least one employee in any calendar quarter during the previous or current year, or,
- At least one employee worked at least part of one day in any 20 or more different weeks of the previous or current year.

The filing must be postmarked on or before the last day of January for the tax year ended the previous December. An approximate two week extension of the filing date is automatically granted if all FUTA deposits were made when due.

Part 1, lines 1a, 1b and 2
Part 1 of Form 940 is intended to capture information regarding state unemployment payments. Boxes 1a, 1b are used to identify the states in which the employer was required to pay state-mandated unemployment tax. Box 1a is to be completed with the postal service state abbreviation code if tax was paid only to a single state. Box 1b is to be checked if unemployment taxes were paid to multiple states. Box 2 is to be checked if any of the states to which state-mandated unemployment tax was paid is classified as a credit reduction state as identified by the U.S. Department of Labor. A credit reduction state is one in which amounts have been borrowed, but not yet repaid, from the federal government in order to pay unemployment benefits. Employers who pay unemployment taxes to a credit reduction state may be subject to additional FUTA taxes.

Schedule A
Schedule A of Form 940 has two purposes as follows:
1. To identify each of the multiple states to which state-mandated unemployment tax was paid and report information regarding wages and taxes paid, and,
2. To calculate and report the amount of credit reduction which is reportable if unemployment taxes were paid to a state that is deemed by the U.S. Department of Labor to be a credit reduction state.

Part 2, lines 3-8
Part 2 of Form 940 is intended to disclose the determination of FUTA taxes due before adjustments. Line 3 is used for the total of all payment amounts to employees such as

- 54 -

compensation, certain fringe benefits, retirement/pension contributions and any other payments. Line 4 is used for the amount of payments reported on line 3 that are excludable from FUTA tax, such as certain fringe benefits, group term life insurance, retirement/pension contributions and dependent care, among others. Check-off boxes 4a-4e are used to indicate the type of expenses included on Line 4. Line 5 is used to report the amount of payments that exceeds the FUTA wage base which is defined as the first $7,000 in payments. Line 5 is calculated as the Line 3 amount, less the Line 4 amount, less $7,000 per employee. Line 6 is the sum of Lines 4 and 5. Line 7 is the difference between Lines 6 and 3 and represents the total amount of wages subject to FUTA tax (which should be no greater than $7,000 per employee). Line 8 represents the actual amount of tax due which is calculated as the product of Line 7 (wages subject to tax) and .006 (or .6%).

Part 3, lines 9-11
Part 3 of Form 940 is intended to determine the amount of adjustments, if any, which are applicable to the amount of FUTA tax determined in Part 2. Line 9 is used to determine additional FUTA taxes due for employers who do not pay unemployment taxes in any state. The calculation is .054 (or 5.4%) of the amount on line 5 (the amounts in excess of $7,000). Line 10 is used for employers who paid some amount of unemployment tax to a state and requires the completion of a detailed worksheet available in the instructions. The worksheet amount represents the additional FUTA tax due as a result of not paying some state amounts. Line 11 represents the credit reduction determined from Schedule A of Form 940 due to making tax payments to a state that was deemed by the U.S. Department of Labor to be a credit reduction state.

Part 4, lines 12-15
Part 4 is intended to compare the FUTA tax that is due with the periodic deposits made throughout the year. Line 12 is the sum of all FUTA liability amounts from Lines 8 through 11. Line 13 is used to report the FUTA deposits made including any overpayments from a prior year. Line 14 is the excess of taxes due over deposits made, representing the net balance due. Line 15 is the excess of deposits made over taxes due, representing the overpayment available for refund or application to a future return.

Part 5, lines 16-17
Part 5 is intended to reconcile the annual liability determined on Line 12 with the sum of the quarterly amounts. Lines 16a and 16d are used to indicate each of the liability amounts that existed for each of the calendar quarters. Note that the total of lines 16a and 16d is entered on Line 17 and must be the same as line 12.

Form 941

Form 941 must be filed by any employer who pays wages. After the first return of an employer is filed, a return is required to be filed in each subsequent quarter regardless of whether or not any wages are paid, unless a so-called final return is filed. Special rules apply to employers of seasonal, household or farm employees. The due date for each Form 941 is generally the end of the month which follows the end of each quarter. However, if all amounts due are timely deposited in the quarter, an automatic extension of 10 days is added to the filing due date. Employers who choose to file electronically are not required to also file returns in paper form. It is important to note that regardless of whether the Form 941 is filed electronically or in paper form, all tax deposits must be made electronically using the Electronic Federal Tax Payment System (EFTPS).

Schedule B

Schedule B of Form 941 is intended to reconcile the tax liability amount for so-called semiweekly depositors. An employer is classified as a semiweekly depositor if one of two conditions is present:

- No less than $50,000 in employment taxes are reported in the look-back period, or,
- An accumulated tax liability of no less than $10,000 exists on any given day in the current or previous calendar year.

The term semiweekly refers to the frequency of tax deposits required of the employer, not the frequency of the payment period to employees. Schedule B is required to be filed by qualifying employers in accompaniment with the corresponding Form 941.

Part 1, lines 1-4

Part 1 of Form 941 is intended to report employee income and withholding amounts for the calendar quarter. Line 1 is used to report the total number of employees who received some sort of wage payment during the quarter. The actual day of determination is specified by the IRS and remained the twelfth day of the last month of each quarter for the calendar year 2016. Line 2 is used to report the total amount of wages, tips and other compensation paid to the employees reported in Line 1. Line 3 is the amounts withheld for income taxes from the amounts paid on Line 2.

Part 1, lines 5a-5f

Lines 5a through 5d are used to calculate the combined employee and employer share of social security and Medicare taxes due for the calendar quarter (not the amount actually withheld). Column 1 is used for the wage base and Column 2 is used for the product of Column 1 multiplied by the tax rate, as indicated on the form. Line 5e is the sum of all taxes due as calculated in Column 2, and Line 5f is used if necessary for the amount of tax due on unreported tips.

Part 1, lines 6-10

Line 6 of Form 941 is the total amount of income and employment taxes due for the quarter, prior to any adjustments, and is calculated as the sum of Lines 3, 5e and 5f. Line 7 is used to report any amount of rounding adjustments between the actual social security and Medicare tax due and the amounts withheld from employees. Line 8 is used to report any adjustments required if sick pay is paid to an employee and social security and Medicare taxes withheld, by a third party. Line 9 is used to report any adjustments resulting from the lack of withholding of social security and Medicare taxes on tips due to the lack of available funds, or the lack of such withholding on group term life insurance premiums paid for former employees. Line 10 is used to report the total amount of taxes due after adjustments and is calculated as the sum of Lines 6 through 9.

Part 1, lines 11-15

Line 11 of Form 941 is used to report the total amount of actual funds deposited for the liabilities of the reported quarter and should include any overpayments from Forms 941-X or 944-X. Line 12a is used to report any COBRA assistance payments provided to eligible employees. In the event such assistance is provided, Line 12b is used to report the number of employees who received such assistance. Line 13 is used to report the total amount of deposits and credits to be applied to the tax liability for the quarter. If the liability from Line 10 is greater than the deposits and credits available on Line 13, a balance is due and is

- 56 -

reported on Line 14. If the amount of deposits and credits on Line 10 is greater than the liability on Line 10, an overpayment has occurred and is to be reported on Line 15.

Part 2, line 16
Part 2 of Form 941 is intended to reconcile the actual quarterly deposit activity with the amount reported on Line 10. Monthly depositors must report the liability for each month in the box provided. Semiweekly depositors are required to complete Schedule B of Form 941 to report the multiple deposits made within each month.

Form 941X

Form 941X, Adjusted *Employer's Quarterly Federal Tax Return or Claim for Refund,* is required to be filed whenever an error is detected on a previously filed Form 941, using a separate Form 941X for each Form 941 that is to be corrected. The general rule for the filing deadline is to file Form 941-X by the due date for the return in the quarter in which the error is discovered. For example, if an error for the third quarter of the previous year is discovered in the first quarter of the following year, Form 941X should be filed by the end of April which is the due date for the first quarter return. Under-reported amounts will not be assessed penalties and/or interest if received as indicated above. Over-reported amounts can be used as credit against a current quarterly return or a request for refund can be filed. Form 941X can be filed any time before three years have passed (the limitation period) since the original return was filed.

Form 943

Employers of agricultural workers are required to file Form 943, *Employer's Annual Federal Tax Return for Agricultural Employees,* if either of the following two conditions is satisfied:
- Any employee is paid no less than $150 in a year, or
- The total wages paid to all employees no less than $2,500.

Employers who meet the criteria above are required to withhold federal income, social security and Medicare taxes from the amounts paid to the employees and file Form 943 no later than the end of January for the preceding calendar year. An automatic extension of approximately ten days is available if all previously required deposits were made timely and the total liability is satisfied. If the total liability for the year is less than $2,500, the amount to be paid may be included with the return. For amounts no less than $2,500, the payments must be made periodically by electronic funds transfer.

Form 944

Form 944, *Employer's Annual Federal Tax Return*, is file by so-called smallest employers who have been notified by the Internal Revenue Service (IRS) that Form 944 can be used on an annual basis rather than Form 941 on a quarterly basis. Form 944 must be filed even if no taxes are due unless the employer has previously filed a final return. The due date for filing is the end of January for the preceding calendar year unless the liability has been paid in full by timely deposits, in which case an automatic extension of approximately 10 days is granted. Employers who are not entitled to use Form 944 are those who have not been notified by the IRS that Form 944 is allowed or those employers who employ household workers or agricultural workers.

Form 945

Form 945, *Annual Return of Withheld Federal Income Tax*, must be filed by payers of certain amounts from which withholdings are made which are not includable as payroll payments. These so-called non-payroll payments include such items as pensions, military retirement, gambling winnings, Indian gaming profits withholding on certain government payments and back-up withholding. The payment amounts from which the withholding is made are required to be reported using certain Forms 1099. Form 945 is not to be used for reporting withholding on wages reportable on Form W-2 and is required to be filed no later than the last day of January for the preceding year. If the entire liability is satisfied with timely deposits, an automatic extension of approximately 10 days is granted.

Form 1042

Form 1042, *Annual Withholding Tax Return for U.S. Source Income of Foreign Persons*, is required to be filed by any withholding agent or intermediary who receives or controls periodic or annual income that meets any one of the following three criteria:
- Form 1042-S is required to be filed, or
- Gross investment income is paid to taxable foreign private foundations, or
- Specified federal procurement payments are paid to any foreign person

Form 1042 is required to be filed no later than March 15 for the preceding year. The time to file can be extended by using Form 7004 but all amounts due must be made by the previous filing deadline.

Form 1042-S

Form 1042-S, *Foreign Person's U.S. Source Income Subject to Withholding*, must be filed by any withholding agent who makes a certain payment as part of a trade or business to an individual who is defined as a foreign person and for which withholding is required. The payments to be reported and amounts withheld include such items as interest on deposits, corporate distributions, rents, royalties and annuities, among others. A foreign person is defined as a nonresident alien individual, fiduciary or foreign corporation. Five copies of Form 1042-S are required to be filed as follows:
- Copy A – filed with the Internal Revenue Service (IRS).
- Copies B, C, D – filed with (distributed to) the recipient.
- Copy E – retained by the payer.

Form 1042-T

Form 1042-T, *Annual Summary and Transmittal of Forms 1042-S*, is to be filed along with the Forms 1042-S, *Foreign Person's U.S. Source Income Subject to Withholding* as the transmittal document. Up to 249 Forms 1042-S may be filed (along with Form 1042-T) in paper form. If 250 or more forms are to be filed, the process must be electronic, in which case form 1042-T is no longer required. The paper copy of Form 1042-T and copy A of the corresponding Forms 1042-S are to be filed with the Ogden Service Center of the Internal Revenue Service no later than March 15 for the preceding year.

Form 1096

Form 1096, *Annual Summary and Transmittal of U.S. Information Returns*, is the transmittal document for the paper filing of Forms W-2G, 1097, 1098, 1099, 3921, 3922 or 5498 and is applicable if less than 250 such forms are to be filed. If the number of forms is no less than 250, the filing must be electronic. Form 1096 must be filed by any person or entity that makes a payment which is required to be reported using Forms W-2G, 1097, 1098, 1099, 3921, 3922 or 5498. Form 1096 is required to be filed with the Internal Revenue Service (based upon the state of residence of the payer) no later than the end of February for the preceding year, except for information relating to an underlying Form 5498 in which case the due date is the end of May.

Form 1099-R

Form 1099-R, *Distributions From Pensions, Annuities, Retirement or Profit Sharing Plans, IRAs, Insurance Contracts, etc.*, must be filed by any person or entity that makes a payment that is a distribution from a plan of no less than $10. Six copies of Form 1099-R are available for filing as follows:
- Copy A – filed with the Internal Revenue Service (IRS).
- Copies B, C and 2 – filed with (distributed to) the recipient.
- Copy D – retained by the payer.
- Copy 1 – filed with the state and/or local entity (if required)

Form 1099-R must be filed with a corresponding Form 1096, *Annual Summary and Transmittal of U.S. Information Returns*. Copy A is must be filed with the IRS no later than the end of February for the preceding year. If the filing is electronic (based on the 250 threshold), the due date to the IRS is the end of March for the preceding year. Copies B, C and 2 must be distributed to the recipient no later than the end of January for the preceding year.

Form 1099-MISC

Form 1099-MISC, *Miscellaneous Income*, is required to be filed by any individual or entity that pays at least $10 in royalties or at least $600 in aggregate for various other items such as rents, services and awards. Copy A of Form 1099-MISC is to be filed with the Internal Revenue Service by the end of February (end of March if filed electronically) for the preceding year and must be accompanied by the corresponding Form 1096. Copy B is to be filed with (distributed to) the recipient by the end of January for the preceding year.

Form 4070

Form 4070, *Employee's Report of Tips to Employer*, is required to be filed by any employee who receives not less than $20 in tips in any given month to an employer, for each month in which the threshold is met. Form 4070 is required to be filed by the tenth day of the month following the month in which at least $20 in tips was received.

Form 8027

Form 8027, *Employer's Annual Information Return of Tip Income and Allocated Tips*, must be filed by so-called large food or beverage establishments in which employees receive income

from tips. A large food or beverage establishment is one in which all of the following criteria are met:
- Food and/or beverage is provided by the establishment for consumption on the premises, and,
- Tipping is a customary practice, and,
- A total of more than 10 employees worked more than 80 hours on a typical business day during the preceding calendar year.

Form 8027 is required to be filed with the Internal Revenue Service (IRS) for each establishment no later than the end of February for the preceding year

EFTPS

Effective January 1, 2011, the Treasury Department eliminated the processing of paper payment vouchers and required that all employer tax payments be deposited electronically using the Electronic Federal Tax Payment System (EFTPS). All depository taxes are subject to this requirement and include the following:
- Corporate income
- Estimated income
- Excise
- Unemployment (FUTA)
- Withholding from foreign corporations and nonresident aliens
- Estimated taxes of certain trusts

The two options for using the EFTPS are as follows:
1. EFTPS Direct (using an ACH Debit) – enrolled employers can access the EFTPS directly and make deposits up until 8pm Eastern Time the day before the deposit is due. EFTPS will then initiate an ACH debit from the account authorized by the employer and deposit to the U.S. Treasury account.
2. EFTPS Through a Financial Institution – employers instruct a designated financial institution to originate an ACH debit on its behalf under the same timing and processing requirements as the direct method.

It is important to note that the employer retains the liability for timely deposits even when using the service of a financial institution. Employers who have a Form 941 liability of less than $2,500 or a Form 944 liability of no more than $1,000 are exempt from the EFTPS depository requirements. Employers with liabilities greater than these amounts must file electronically, even if a third party service is required to facilitate the actual transfer of funds.

Penalties for failure to deposit on time

Penalties for failure to deposit timely without reasonable cause are as follows:
- Within 5 Days of the Due Date: 2% of the undeposited amount.
- Within 6-15 Days of the Due Date: 5% of the undeposited amount.
- More Than 15 Days After the Due Date: 10% of the undeposited amount.
- More Than 15 Days After the Due Date and More Than 10 Days After Receipt of an Internal Revenue Service (IRS) Delinquency Notice: 15% of the undeposited amount.

Look-back period

The look-back period is used by employers to determine the required frequency of depositing employment taxes. The look-back period for a particular calendar year for an employer that files Form 941, *Employer's Quarterly Federal Tax Return* is defined as the 12-month period ending the previous June 30. For example, the look-back period for the year 2016 is the 12-month period from July 1, 2014 to June 30, 2015. The look-back period for a particular calendar year for an employer that files form 944, *Employer's Annual Federal Tax Return*, is defined as the calendar year ended two Decembers prior. For example, the look-back period for the year 2016 is the calendar year ended December 31, 2014. The amount of total employment tax liability in the look-back period determines whether or not the employer must deposit taxes either monthly or semiweekly. As of 2016, the threshold amount remains $50,000. Employers with a liability no greater than the threshold must deposit monthly; those with a liability greater than $50,000 must deposit semiweekly.

Monthly and semimonthly depositors of employment taxes

An employer with a look-back period liability of no greater than $50,000 is designated as a monthly depositor and is required to deposit the total employment tax liability for a calendar month no later than the 15th day of the following month. An employer with a look-back period liability of greater than $50,000 is designated as a semiweekly depositor and is required to deposit the total employment tax liability for a calendar week as follows:
- For wages paid on Saturday through Tuesday – deposit date is the following Friday.
- For wages paid on Wednesday through Friday – deposit date is the following Wednesday.

One-day deposit rule

The one-day deposit rule requires any employer who accumulates no less than $100,000 by any day during the deposit period must deposit the funds no later than the end of the next banking day. For example, a monthly depositor who accumulates a $100,000 liability before the last day of the month must deposit the funds by the end of the next banking day. Thereafter, the employer automatically becomes a semiweekly depositor. For a semiweekly depositor, any accumulated liability of $100,000 or more during either of the semiweekly periods (Saturday through Tuesday, or Wednesday through Friday) must deposit the funds by the end of the next banking day.

Quarterly and annual deposit rules

The quarterly "de minimis" deposit rule allows employers who accumulate a total employment tax liability of less than $2,500 in any quarter to deposit the amount in conjunction with the filing of the Form 941, *Employer's Quarterly Federal Tax Return,* rather than during the normal monthly or semiweekly period. The annual de minimis deposit rule allows employers who accumulate a total employment tax liability of no more than $1,000 in a calendar year to deposit the amount in conjunction with the filing of the Form 944, *Employer's Annual Federal Tax Return.* Employers who so qualify are typically not required to deposit either monthly or semiweekly.

Shortfall rule

The shortfall rule refers to small underpayments upon which penalties will not be applied. This so-called "safe harbor" rule is applied if the underpayment is no greater than $100 or no greater than 2% of the amount due, whichever amount is larger. The original deposit must have been made by the due date and the shortfall must be paid as follows:
- For monthly depositors, by the due date of the quarterly return (Form 941).
- For semiweekly depositors, by first Wednesday or Friday due date after the 15th of the month.

Deposit requirements for sick pay administered by a third party

The deposit rules for taxes withheld from employees on sick pay that is administered by a third party are the same as for regular wages. The liability for deposit begins at the point that the amounts are withheld. However, the liability for depositing the employer share of social security and Medicare depends upon which party is responsible for the deposit, the third party or the employer. If the third party does not transfer liability to the employer, the third party is responsible for making the deposit along with the employee withholding. If the third party transfers the responsibility to the employer, the employer is responsible for the deposit and the time period begins at the point of timely notification.

Substantiation rules for charitable contributions

In order for charitable contributions to be deductible from income for federal tax purposes, the taxpayer must be prepared to substantiate the contribution in the form of "contemporaneous written acknowledgement." For contributions that are made using a payroll deduction method with an employer, the Internal Revenue Service (IRS) has interpreted the substantiation rules such that the written acknowledgement requirement is satisfied if both of the following are present:
- A payroll check stub, Form W-2 or some other employer provided document that indicates the amount withheld for the charitable contribution, and,
- A document is provided by the receiving charity that indicates that no goods or services were exchanged for the contribution from the employee.

Reporting tips to employers

Employees are required to report cash (or credit card) tips received from customers if no less than $20 is received in any month while working for a single employer. If an employee works for more than one employer but receives less than $20 with each employer, no tips are required to be reported. Form 4070, *Employee's Report of Tips to Employer,* can be used for purposes of reporting but employers may also use any other type of reporting mechanism. Employees are required to report to the employer by the 10th day of the month following the month in which the tips were received.

Withholding requirements for tip income

Tip income that is reported to the employer is subject to withholding for income, social security and Medicare taxes and must be withheld from the regular wages of the employee. If the amount of regular wages is insufficient to provide for full withholding, the employer can request an additional payment from the employee. If a liability still remains after withholding and employee request, the accumulated amount unpaid must be reported on the Form W-2 of the employee after the end of the year.

General payroll and tax information required by to be retained by employers

<u>IRS requirements</u>
The general rule for records to be retained by the IRS include all gross-to-net information for each employee from each payroll period in a calendar year and the related filed tax returns using Forms 941, 943, 944, 945, 941-X, W-2, W-3. In addition, the following information is also required to be retained:
- Employee Form W-4.
- Documentation of reported tips by employees.
- Information regarding wage continuation payments including Form W-4S.
- Fringe benefits provided including required substantiation.
- Cumulative wage withholding method requests.
- Tax deposit information.
- Annuity payment information.
- Employee personal information (address, social security number, etc.)
- Employer information (address, EIN, etc.)

The retention period for the above information is four years after the due date of the applicable tax returns (employee and employer).

The retention requirements generally apply to tip income and benefit plans. However, the following exceptions apply:
- Records that substantiate allocated tip income by an employer to employees must be maintained for three years after the due date of the corresponding return.
- Records of benefit plans that are required to substantiate the pre-tax qualification of the plan must be kept as long as necessary to provide such substantiation.

<u>Department of Labor requirements</u>
FLSA: Employers are required by the FLSA to retain the following information:
- Retained for at least three years
  - o Collective bargaining agreements, certificates authorizing employment of certain types of employees, total sales volume and goods purchased.
  - o For each employee,
    - Name (corresponding to social security card, address, date of birth, sex, occupation.
    - Time and day of beginning of work week, regular rate and basis of pay, hours worked each work day and work week, straight time earnings, overtime earnings.
    - Additions to, deductions from pay, total wages paid each pay period, data of payment and pay period.
- Retained for at least two years
  - o Basic employment and earnings records for each employee.
  - o Order, shipping and billing records for sales volume and goods purchased.
  - o Records substantiating additions to or deductions from employee wages paid.

Since white collar employees are exempt from the minimum wage and overtime provisions mandated by the FLSA (so-called exempt employees), the records requirement includes only regular rate and basis of pay, hours worked, straight time earnings, overtime pay (if any), and deductions from wages. The records must be sufficient as to calculate the total earnings per period for each employee.

FMLA: The record retention requirements of the Department of Labor under the Family Medical Leave Act (FMLA) are as follows:
- Employee and basic payroll data such as name, address, occupation, rate or basis of pay, terms of compensation, hours worked (daily, weekly), additions to and deductions from pay.
- Dates of FMLA leave taken or hours of leave if taken incrementally.
- Copies of notices between employer and employee.
- Documents related to employee practices for paid and unpaid leave.
- Records of any dispute between employer and employee related to FMLA.

The FMLA requires that medical records be segregated from other employee records and treated in a confidential manner as for all other medical records. However, certain exceptions are provided as follows:
- Information regarding the provision of needed accommodations to the employee can be disclosed to the supervisor of the employee.
- Information regarding the medical condition of the employee can be disclosed to first aid and safety personnel in case of emergency treatment.
- Information requested by FMLA government compliance personnel can be disclosed as requested.

State requirements
The general payroll information required to be retained by most states in accordance with unemployment insurance and wage and hour laws is as follows:

Unemployment Insurance Laws	Wage and Hour Laws
Name, social security number	Name, address
Dates of hire, separation, rehire, reinstatement after layoff	Position, hours worked each day, week
Compensation paid each payroll period	Compensation paid each payroll period
Payroll periods and dates	Rate of pay
Date and reason for termination	Age of employee (if a minor)
Time lost due to employee unavailability	

The retention period varies by state and ranges from no specified date (in multiple states) to seven years (in Tennessee).

ADEA requirements
In addition to records required to be retained by other regulations, the Age Discrimination in Employment Act (ADEA) requires retention by employers of records that are related to various personnel actions such as the following:
- Job applications, resumes, or other advertisement responses.
- Failure to hire an individual.
- Promotion, demotion, transfer, selection for training, layoff, recall or discharge.

- 64 -

- Job orders submitted to employment agencies.
- Tests or physical exams, job advertisements.

Unemployment tax information required to be retained by employers

Employers are required to retain the following FUTA records for at least four years after the due date of the corresponding Form 940 *Employer's Annual Federal Unemployment (FUTA) Tax Return:*
- Total employee compensation paid during the calendar year.
- The amount of total employee compensation that is subject to FUTA tax.
- The amount of state unemployment contributions categorized as either withheld or not withheld from wages.
- All Form 940 information.
- Explanatory information for differences between total and taxable compensation, if any.

Documentation of proof of identity and authorization to work

The U.S. Citizenship and Immigration Services (USCIS) requires documentation of proof of identity and authorization to work. Employees are required to complete Form I-9 *Employment Eligibility Verification* and employers are required to retain the form for at least three years after the date of hire, or at least one year after the date of termination, whichever is latest. The information that the employee must provide to substantiate the Form I-9 is one document that proves both identity and authorization to work (such as a passport or permanent resident card from so-called List A) or one form that proves identity (from so-called List B) and a separate from that proves authorization (from so-called List C). The specific documents are listed on flashcard #002.

Penalties for noncompliance with IRS record keeping rules

The failure to comply with IRS record keeping rules may result in the issuance of a *Notice of Inadequate Records* to the taxpayer which can subsequently lead to penalty assessments such as:
- Accuracy-related civil penalties
- Willful failure criminal penalties

The fine for criminal penalties can be as much as $25,000 for an individual and $100,000 for a corporation, and/or imprisonment for up to one year. In addition, the taxpayer may be liable for the costs of prosecution.

Penalties for noncompliance with DOL record keeping rules

The penalty for noncompliance with Department of Labor (DOL) record keeping rules can be as much as a $10,000 fine and/or imprisonment for as long as six months. However, the costs of faulty record keeping can be much higher if the lack of records prevents an employer from refuting evidence and testimony brought in a lawsuit. Lacking the records, a plaintiff will often prevail in that the information offered (by the employee) will be accepted.

Additional penalties for faulty record keeping

In addition to penalties for faulty record keeping, a taxpayer who is unable to substantiate transactions due to a lack of records can be assessed penalties for inadequate withholding, underpayment of taxes, late filing of statements and returns and various other violations.

Penalties for hiring or continuing to employ unauthorized aliens

Except for certain minor and unintentional procedural violations, employers who knowingly hire or continue to employ unauthorized aliens are subject to a series of graduating fines based upon the number of offenses under the U.S. Citizenship and Immigration Service (USCIS):
- First Offense: $3,200 per worker
- Second Offense: up to $6,500 per worker
- More Than Two Offenses: up to $16,000 per worker

Additional fines are levied when employers fail to follow the verification requirements ($110-$1,100 per worker) and, if a pattern and practice of noncompliance is determined, criminal penalties and imprisonment can be assessed. An employer can be found to have "knowingly" hired and continued to employ an unauthorized alien if it is determined by the Immigration and Customs Enforcement bureau (ICE) that the employer had either actual or constructive knowledge that the employee was unauthorized. Actual or constructive knowledge is interpreted to mean that the employer either knew or should have known the facts in question.

Calculation of the Paycheck

Total remuneration and regular rate of pay

Total remuneration under the FLSA includes all payments "for employment paid to, or on behalf of, the employee." That said, the FLSA excludes certain types of payments including gifts, business expense reimbursements, and matching payments to employee retirement plans. The FLSA defines regular rate of pay as the "regular hourly rate of pay of an employee...determined by dividing his total remuneration for employment (except statutory exclusions) in any workweek by the total number of hours actually worked by him in that workweek for which such compensation was paid."

Workweek and hours worked

Under the FLSA, an "employee's workweek is a fixed and regularly recurring period of 168 hours - seven consecutive 24-hour periods. It need not coincide with the calendar week but may begin on any day and at any hour of the day." This time period becomes the standard to determine if overtime is due the employee. The FLSA requires that an employee must be paid for all hours worked. The FLSA does not define the term "work" but court cases and legislation subsequent to the enactment of the FLSA define it as being time on duty at a prescribed place as well as certain activities occurring before or after an employee is considered to be at his or her workplace.

Regular rate of pay

The formula for calculating the regular rate of pay is: amount of pay/number of hours worked (not including overtime). Here are some examples using the formula to calculate regular rate of pay: 1) Gene Simmons was paid $350 for working 40 hours in one week at the Office Shack selling office supplies. His pay rate can be figured by dividing $350 by 40, which results in $8.75 per hour. 2) Jane Thomas works at the law firm of Scott, Deal and McGraw as a legal secretary. She was paid $550 for working 40 hours per week. Her regular rate of pay is $13.75 per hour, which is determined by dividing $550 by 40.

Overtime pay

Here are some examples of calculating overtime pay: 1) Jane Krill is a reporter for "The Night Owl." Last week, she worked 48 hours at an hourly rate of $10 per hour. Her first 40 hours would be paid at $10 per hour (40 hr x $10/hr = $400.00). The other 8 hours would be paid at $15.00 per hour (1.5 x $10/hr), (8 hr x $15.00 = $120.00). Total pay for the workweek would be $520.00. ($400.00 + $120.00). 2) Helen Dill makes $8 per hour working as a car wash attendant for Clean Car. She worked 50 hours last week. Her first 40 hours would be paid at $8.00 per hour (40 hr x $8.00/hr = $320). The other 10 hours would be paid at $12.00 per hour (1.5 overtime rate x $8.00/hr). Harriet's overtime pay is $120.00. Her total pay for the workweek would be $440.00 ($320 + $120 = $440).

Calculating overtime pay where remuneration for an employee includes housing
Suppose the employee's remuneration includes housing valued at $400 per month. The value of the housing must be added to the employee's total wages for the workweek in

order to calculate the regular rate of pay. The employee worked 44 hours at a rate of $10 per hour. To determine the effective regular rate of pay, the housing must be converted to an annual amount, and that amount divided by 52. So if we multiply the monthly housing value by 12 ($400 x 12 = $4,800) and divide by 52 ($4,800 / 52 = $92.31), we can add that amount to the employee's total remuneration. Multiply the straight-time wage rate times the number of hours actually worked during the workweek ($10 x 44 = $440) and add the value of the housing ($440 + $92.31 = $532.31). Divide the total by the hours actually worked during the workweek to determine the effective regular rate of pay ($532.31 / 44 = $12.10). Multiply this rate times 1.5 to determine the overtime rate ($18.15), and multiply this rate time the number of hours worked in excess of 40 to determine the overtime pay ($72.60) Going one step further, total pay would equal straight-time pay ($12.10 x 40 = $484.00) plus overtime pay ($72.60), or $556.60.

Calculating overtime premium for an employee paid only by commission
Suppose an employee is paid $1,000 commission during a 50-hour workweek. His pay is $1,000/50 = $20/hr. Overtime premium is 10 hr x 0.5 x $20 =$100.

Calculating overtime premium with a housing allowance
Assume the calculated regular rate of pay, including housing allowance, is $12.10 on 44 hours worked during the workweek. The overtime premium is calculated at one-half the regular rate times the number of hours worked in excess of 40 ($6.05 x 4 = $24.20). Going one step further, total pay would equal the straight-time portion of pay on all hours worked (44 x $12.10 = $532.40) plus the overtime premium ($24.20), or $556.60.

Holiday premium pay

Holiday premium pay is sometimes called "double time." An employee who works a holiday is entitled by many entities to pay at his or her rate of basic pay plus premium pay at a rate equal to his or her rate of basic pay for non-overtime hours worked up to 8, except that an employee on a compressed (not flexible) schedule may be paid holiday pay for all non-overtime hours worked for that day. Holiday premium pay is not overtime pay. An employee who works overtime on a holiday gets the same overtime rate he or she would get on any other day for overtime hours worked. Multiply hourly rate by number of non-overtime hours worked on holiday (not to exceed 8 hours or the number of non-overtime hours in a compressed schedule).

Grossing up net amounts

Calculating the gross equivalent of a net amount is called "grossing up." Why Gross-up? Some typical circumstances for grossing up include the following situations:
- An employee receives a $1,000 bonus. The sales manager wants the salesperson to receive $1,000 in cash (after withholding taxes), so the gross bonus will be more than $1,000.
- The employer pays the employee's taxes on taxable relocation expenses.
- The value of a taxable benefit for a terminated employee is calculated but social security tax or Medicare tax was not withheld; gross-up is required. When grossing up, the taxes paid by the employer are included in the employee's taxable income.

To calculate gross-up, take the following steps:
- 100% - tax% (federal/state/local taxes) = Net%
- Payment /Net% = Gross amount of earnings
- Check by calculating gross to net pay

When grossing up a check, one should be mindful of the "pyramiding effect." Depending on the reason for grossing up, additional grossing up calculations may be necessary to offset any related increases in employee taxable income.

Payments after the death of an employee

A payroll office might have different procedures for paying survivors of employees upon the death of the employee. Here are some sample procedures which might be used: 1) any payments in process after the date of death should be stopped, returned to the employer, or both. 2) Termination paperwork and adjustment vouchers should be completed and routed to the appropriate offices. 3) The family of the deceased should be given instructions for claiming final payments to employees. 4) Any outstanding checks issued to the deceased with dates prior to the date of death must be voided and reissued to the survivor.

Workers' compensation

When an employee is injured at work, his or her claim is filed with the insurance company or self-insuring employer, who will pay 100% of the employee's "reasonable and necessary" medical bills, plus disability benefits according to the particular state's approved formula. In most states, the employee will receive 2/3 of their average weekly wage for the period that they are unable to work due to the injury. If the employee is only able to work part time, their wage loss benefits will be adjusted accordingly. There is generally no benefit available for pain and suffering (offsetting the fact that workers' compensation is generally a "no fault" system), but workers are paid according to the extent and duration of the disability.

The following are worker's compensation terms:
- The average Weekly Wage (AWW): The AWW is one method by which entitlement to wage loss benefits may be calculated. Average weekly earnings for a fixed period of time are calculated and wage loss benefits are calculated based on that amount.
- The average daily wage (ADW) is another calculation of an injured employee's average earnings for wage loss benefits determination and may be useful when the AWW would not be appropriate.
- An independent medical examination (IME) is a medical examination conducted by independent medical personnel (not affiliated with any of the parties to the claim), required by the employer or insurer to determine the existence, nature, and extent of the employee's injuries pursuant to their rights under litigation.

Club membership as part of employee benefits

Club dues are taxable income to the employee, except for that portion of the dues that are related to business. These may be country clubs, golf or airline clubs. The portion of the club dues considered personal income to the employee can be treated as a wage expense by the employer. Here is an example: James Miles belongs to the Sky High Club. It is a traveler's club that allows members into exclusive clubs at airports, both domestically and abroad.

James estimates that he uses these facilities about 60 percent of the time while traveling because of company-related matters. His travel records back up his contentions. The annual membership cost is $800. Accordingly, only 40 percent of the cost, or $320, can be accounted for as James' personal income.

Overtime worked during vacation

When employees work overtime during a week in which they also take vacation, vacation pay may be omitted from the regular rate computation as long as it is reasonably equivalent to the amount the employee normally earns during a similar time period. The FLSA does not allow vacation pay to be used as a credit against overtime pay, however. In general, the employer should calculate pay for time actually worked, and then add vacation pay to that amount.

Qualified and non-qualified employee retirement plans and defined-benefit plans

A qualified plan is eligible for certain tax benefits not available to a nonqualified plan. Qualified plans must be for the exclusive benefit of employees or their beneficiaries, and they are subject to Internal Revenue Code requirements; nonqualified plans are an agreement or promise by an employer to certain employees, or a certain class of employees, to provide benefits at a future date for services currently performed. Qualified plans may be either defined benefit plans or defined contribution plans. A defined benefit plan is employer-sponsored, and benefits are formula-based. The employer controls portfolio risk and management.

Entertainment tickets as employee benefit income

Tickets to sporting events, concerts, and other entertainment events are fringe benefits and should be reported as employee gross income. The amount reported should be calculated by subtracting employee costs and tax deductions related to the benefit from the fair market value of the benefit.

Deferred compensation plans

Deferred compensation plans are those in which employees can accumulate money on a tax-deferred basis. A qualified plan may allow employee withdrawals without penalty for certain "emergency" situations specified in the plan, although consideration should be given to tax issues related to withdrawals such as regular income taxation, early withdrawal penalties, and ten-year lump-sum tax treatment. Some plans may allow the employee to take the benefit in cash. A deferred compensation plan can be combined with other plans; a 401(k) plan is a type of employer-sponsored deferred compensation plan.

Defined-contribution retirement plan

In a defined-contribution retirement plan, the employer sets aside a certain amount or percentage of money each year for the benefit of the employee. An employee will have no way of knowing how much he or she will ultimately receive from the plan. The benefit is not fixed; the amount contributed is.

FSA

A flexible spending account (FSA) is a type of cafeteria plan set up through an employer in the United States. It is a tax-advantaged savings account that allows employees to set aside a portion of their pay to satisfy qualified medical or dependent care expenses. Money deposited into an FSA through payroll deduction is not subject to payroll taxes, resulting in a substantial payroll tax savings. An FSA is similar to the Health Savings Account (HSA) available to self-employed persons or some small businesses. A FSA can save on taxes as well as contribute to health or dependent care. For instance, assume a person in the 28% Federal marginal bracket is subject to a 4% state tax, along with the FICA taxes of 7.65%. Assume also that this person had $2,000 deducted and put into an FSA for health care; this would result in almost $800 in tax savings (28% + 4% + 7.65% = 39.65% x $2,000 = $793). If this person had instead included $2,000 of medical expense on an itemized federal income tax return, he or she would be able to deduct only that portion that exceeds the 7.5% of Adjusted Gross Income threshold.

Cafeteria plan

A cafeteria plan is the generic term for an employee benefit plan that allows employees to select among various group programs that best meet their specific needs. Sometimes these are varying benefit plans or add-ons provided through the same insurer or third party administrator, other times this refers to the offering of different plans or health maintenance organizations, or HMOs, provided by different managed care or insurance companies. A simple form of cafeteria plan, the premium-only plan, lets employees take employer-required health insurance deductibles from pretax income. It is relatively simple for a company to administer and employees see a small reduction in taxes taken from their checks.

Relocation benefits

Companies are required by the Internal Revenue code to report certain payments or reimbursements of moving and housing expenses as taxable income. Relocation benefits that are not generally taxable include: moving household goods, the first 30 days of storage, and final move travel. Other aspects of relocation, such as temporary housing, are taxable. Some companies will offer to those relocating that taxes be grossed up related to relocation. The term "gross up" means that the company will calculate and pay tax assistance (gross up dollar amount) based on the amount of taxable relocation benefits that have been paid for by the company. The company processes payment of the tax assistance amount directly with the IRS on the employee's behalf.

It can be shown how taxable employee compensation from a relocation benefit is computed by using the following example: A college hire has a total relocation cost of $12,500. The taxable relocation cost is $5,000. Total taxes on relocation costs paid by the company as a gross-up for new hires (the grossed-up amount for federal income tax and FICA) is $1,856 federal income tax, $567.93 Medicare and Old age, Survivors, and Disability insurance, the official name for Social Security. The total taxable compensation on the W-2 is $7,423.91. In the example, the company pays $1,856 to the IRS and $568 FICA paid on the employee's behalf. These figures are calculated on a 7.65% FICA rate and using the federal withholding rate of 25% as a "supplemental" rate from the IRS.

Business expense reimbursement and employee income

If an employee turns in evidence of expenses that can be reimbursed, the payment made by the employer would not be viewed under law as income. The evidence used to substantiate expenses may include: 1) receipts that indicate the expense total. 2) Per diem rates not exceeding those listed by the IRS. Only 50 percent of the costs for meals and entertainment can be deducted by the employer even though the employee may be entitled to the entire amount being reimbursed and not considered income.

Employee stock options

Employee stock options are stock options for the company's own stock that are often offered to upper-level employees as part of the executive compensation package, especially by American corporations. An employee stock option is identical to a call option on the company's stock, with some extra restrictions. A call option is a financial contract between two parties, the buyer and the seller of this type of option. In the U.S., stock options granted to employees are of two forms that differ primarily in their tax treatment. They may be either incentive stock options or non-qualified stock options. The company gives a stock option grant to the employee which specifies:
- The number of options granted to the employee
- The option's exercise price
- The option's expiration date
- The option's vesting schedule, specifying when options may first be exercised
- Restrictions on what can and can't be done with the options

Incentive stock options
Incentive stock options (ISOs), are a type of employee stock option that can be granted only to employees and confer a U.S. tax benefit. The tax benefit is not having to pay ordinary income tax on the difference between the exercise price and the fair market value of the shares issued (however, U.S. alternative minimum tax may be due). For shares held for 1 year from the date of exercise and 2 years from the date of grant, any profit made on sale of the shares is considered long-term capital gain and taxed in the U.S. at lower rates than ordinary income.

Employee stock purchase plans and deductions for plans

Certain companies allow their employees to buy company stock at reduced prices. Those purchases are usually made through deductions from employee pay and are normally capped at a percentage of employee pay. Here is an example: Megamartco offers its employees stock at a 20% discount from the market price of the stock. Employees buy stocks through deductions covering the stock's share cost. Jane Rapp chose to have $10 deducted from her paycheck so she can purchase her company's stock. For the first paycheck in which there is a stock deduction, the publicly-traded price is $17.50 per share, so Jane cannot buy it from the company at the reduced price of $14 ($17.50 market price x 1-20%). The company holds the funds until next payday, at which time the funds available are $20. One share is deposited in Jane's account and $6 is left for the next buy.

Non-qualified stock options

Unlike incentive stock options, non-qualified stock options do not qualify for special tax treatment. On the other hand, incentive stock options require the holder to take on more risk because longer holding periods are required in order to receive better tax treatment. Exercising non-qualified stock options results in taxable income equal to the difference between the exercise price and the market price of the stock at exercise.

Minimum value of employee stock options

A typical employee stock option has time value but no intrinsic value at grant date, but the option is still worth something. Minimum value is the minimum price someone would be willing to pay for the option. The so-called minimum value method derives its name from the theory underlying its calculation. The idea is that a person who wishes to purchase a call option on a given stock would be willing to pay at least (and the option seller would accept at least) an amount representing the benefit (sacrifice) of the right to defer payment of the exercise price until the end of the option's term. Minimum value of an employee stock option can be found by a present value calculation. The current price of the stock is reduced by the present value of any dividends on the stock expected during the option's term, and by the present value of the exercise price. Present values are based on the risk-free rate of return.

Stock award

Some stock-based compensation plans require an employer to pay an employee in cash for the increase in the employer's stock price from a specified level; the payment may be either on demand or at a specified date. The employer must measure compensation cost for the award based on the changes in the stock price in the periods in which the changes occur.

Calculating value of group term life insurance

The value of group term life insurance an employer pays for is excluded from income for the first $50,000 purchased. The excess value must be included in employee income but is only subject to Social Security and Medicare. The IRS has a table to determine the fair market value per $1,000 of group term for a range of age brackets. Here is an example. A 50-year-old employee gets $80,000 of group term insurance through work. He contributes $2 per month to it. The first $50,000 of this amount is excluded from the employee's gross income. To calculate the remaining value:
$30,000/1,000 x $0.23 (as taken from the IRS table for the 50-54 age bracket), = fair market value of $6.90/mo.
$6.90 - employee's $2/mo. contribution = net monthly value received of $4.90.
Next $4.90 x 12 for full year's value = $58.80.
The $58.80 should be reported as the employee's gross income.

De minimis fringe benefits

In general, a de minimis benefit is one for which, considering its value and the frequency with which it is provided, is so small as to make accounting for it unreasonable or impractical. This would include such items as:

- Controlled, occasional employee use of photocopier
- Occasional snacks, coffee, doughnuts, etc.
- Occasional tickets for entertainment events
- Holiday gifts
- Occasional meal money or transportation expense for working overtime
- Group-term life insurance for an employee's spouse or dependents with face value not more than $2,000
- Flowers, fruit, books, etc., provided under special circumstances

In determining whether a benefit is de minimis, one should always consider its frequency and its value. An essential element of a de minimis benefit is that it is occasional or unusual in frequency. It also must not be a form of disguised compensation.

Exclusions
De minimis fringe benefits are excluded from employee taxable income because their value is so small it is unreasonable or administratively impractical for the employer to account for them. They can be in the form of property or service, but cannot be cash or anything easily converted to cash.

Cash and gift certificates
Cash is generally intended as a wage, and usually provides no administrative burden to account for. Cash therefore cannot be a de minimis fringe benefit, with one exception: occasional meal or transportation money to enable an employee to work overtime. The benefit must be provided so that employees can work an unusual, extended schedule. The benefit is not excludable for any regular scheduled hours, even if they include overtime. The employee must actually work the overtime. Meal money calculated on the basis of number of hours worked is not de minimis and is taxable wages. Gift certificates that can be applied only to a choice of one type of item would generally be considered non cash and could be tax-exempt as de minimis benefits. Whether or not a gift certificate is considered equivalent to cash depends on all the facts and circumstances.

Employee educational assistance and employee income

Reimbursing an employee's expenses for education is not income for the employee if the education is being reimbursed and is related to his or her job and will help the employee maintain or improve skills for the job. But the payments are considered income if the education is used for promoting the employee or to shift them to a position that requires different skills that are unrelated to their current job. If the employer has a written educational assistance plan that meets certain conditions, the Internal Revenue Code will allow each of the employees an exemption of $5,250 per year for employer-paid education assistance.

Working condition fringe benefit exclusions

Employers often provide employees with property or services to be used in the performance of their job duties. These items are considered to be working condition fringe benefits when they would be allowable as tax deductible ordinary and necessary business expenses if the employee were to purchase them for use in their job. As working condition fringe benefits, the Internal Revenue Code excludes employer provided property and services from employee taxable income so long as they are used for such business (and not personal) purposes.

Status of award payments as taxable income

According to the Internal Revenue Service, award payments are considered supplemental wages to the employee, subject to certain exclusions. The cash, or fair market value of the goods or services received as a bonus or award, must be included in the employee's Form W-2. Certain awards may be eligible for tax exclusion. For instance, whether employee achievement awards must be included in taxable income depends on several factors, such as length of service, time elapsed since receiving the same award (in the case of a length of service awards), employee's position in the company (in the case of a safety awards), and the dollar amount of the award (subject to whether the award is qualified or nonqualified). The award must be made as part of a meaningful employer presentation, and any award found to be disguised compensation will be considered taxable income regardless of meeting exclusion conditions.

Gross-up an award amount
To calculate the applicable gross amount of an employee award for taxes, add all appropriate tax rates together for a total tax rate and subtract the total tax rate from 100% to calculate the net percentage amount. Divide the net payment by the net percentage; this is the tax "grossed up" amount. This amount must be included on the employee's Form W-2, Wage and Tax Statement. Following is an example of calculating a "gross up" award amount. Herman works for Acme Steam Rollers. His company gave him a $500 performance award for turning out an order for steam rollers 2 days ahead of schedule. He lives in the state of North Atlantic, a fictional state with a state tax rate of 3%. Here is how to gross-up Herman's award amount and figure taxes owed: Federal tax: 25%. State tax: 3%. Medicare tax: 1.45%. Social Security: 6.2%. Total tax rate: 35.65%. Net percentage: 100-35.65 = 64.35%. Net Award: $500. $500/64.35% = $777 gross award. Federal tax = $194.25. State tax = $23.31. Medicare tax = $11.27. Social Security = $48.17. Net amount: $500.

Special Accounting Rule

The Special Accounting Rule refers to the practice of employers deferring reporting of non-cash fringe benefits (employer-provided automobiles, free paid-parking for the employee, and health and life insurance excluding group term life insurance) to employees in the months of November and December to the following tax year. So an employer may wait to report an employer-provided vehicle that was provided in November 2016 until January 2017. This safe harbor practice allowed by the Internal Revenue Service (IRS) assists the employer in preparing and reporting the employee's IRS Form W-2 in a more efficient manner. It also assists the employee by making tax planning more convenient, and does not reduce the employee's take-home pay at year's end. Non-cash fringe benefits are reported on IRS Form W-2 as wages. The special accounting rule may be applied selectively to benefits, but all employees must have this type of reporting if any one employee is reported this way. It is not necessary to notify the IRS that the employer is using this method of reporting, but it is necessary to inform the employees that are affected.

Standard mileage rates

Standard mileage rates are set by the Internal Revenue Service (IRS) to acknowledge the depreciation and use of fuel for vehicles used for purposes that the IRS deems deserving of deduction. For tax year 2016, taxpayers may write off $0.54 per mile driven for business purposes, $0.19 per mile driven for medical or moving purposes, and $0.14 per mile driven on behalf of a charitable organization. The standard mileage rates are used in lieu of depreciation charts, and are calculated based on studies related to the annual costs of operating vehicles. As an alternative to using the standard mileage rate, taxpayers may track actual costs associated with operating their vehicles and use that instead. Many employers reimburse employees mileage at the standard rate. This allows the employee to benefit from the mileage rate immediately, and the employer may write it off as a business expense in that tax year.

Taxation of worker expenses for transit, parking, and commuting

Employees who commute to work may be eligible for certain tax benefits pertaining to expenses incurred related to parking and transit costs. The benefit varies from tax year to tax year, and may be eliminated from law altogether. As of 2016, commuting employees can exclude from their income up to $255 per month in reimbursement for parking expenses incurred, and $255 per month for transit passes and commuter vehicle fees (i.e. subways). (On January 1, 2016, the monthly transit limit was made to be always equal to the monthly limit for parking.) They may also exclude reimbursement for up to $20 per month from their income related to expenses incurred while riding a bicycle to work.

Calculation of federal tax levies

To determine the amount an employee's payroll that is available to be levied for federal tax payments, the payroll department must first tabulate existing payments that supersede tax levies according to law. Existing payments of tax and any child support garnishments are to be withheld from the gross pay of the employee. After these have been considered, the payroll department then subtracts any voluntary deductions at the time that the levy is placed. Based on this number, the payroll professional should locate the amount of the employee's income that is considered exempt according to Internal Revenue Service Publication 1494. IRS Publication 1494 will then direct the payroll department in the appropriate amount to be withheld according to the employee's marital status and the number of exemptions that he or she claims on IRS Form W-4. Also, considered in this amount is the frequency with which the payroll is distributed. The payroll department should subtract this amount and existing voluntary contribution, taxes, and garnishments from the employee's gross pay to determine the amount that it should withhold from an employee's payroll to satisfy the levy.

Calculation of student loan garnishments

In the event that an employee is negligent in the repayment of his or her student loans, federal law allows for the garnishment of wages to help the lender collect what is due.

Student loans are subordinate to tax levies and child support payments, and thus those garnishments have priority of payment. Rules regarding garnishment of wages for student loans vary according to whether the lender is the federal government or a private lender. A private lender will have to obtain a court order to garnish wages, whereas the government does not. The lenders are also different in that the government may only garnish 10% of the employee's disposable income, whereas a private lender may garnish up to 25% of the employee's disposable income. As with other loan garnishments, this percentage may not exceed thirty times the current minimum wage. In this case, disposable wage refers to the amount of an employee's payroll left over after taking all other legally required deductions.

Calculation of creditor garnishments

In the event that an employee is negligent in the satisfaction of his or her debt obligations, federal law allows for the garnishment of wages to help satisfy the debt. Federal law recognizes that heavy garnishments may be counterproductive to the employee's situation, and thus, limits the amount of the employee's payroll that a debtor may garnish. Under federal law, a debtor may garnish up to 25% of an individual's disposable pay, or if the employee's disposable pay exceeds thirty times the current minimum wage, the debtor may garnish that amount, whichever is less. In this case, disposable wage refers to the amount of an employee's payroll left over after taking all other legally required deductions. Additionally, debtor garnishments are subordinated to tax levies and child support payments, and may only be taken after those garnishments are satisfied, if there are any funds left after that.

Calculation for backup withholding

Backup withholding occurs in the event that a taxpayer's personal information with the Internal Revenue Service (IRS) is incorrect, or if the IRS believes that certain types of income received by the taxpayer are being under reported by that taxpayer. The most common informational dispute with the IRS is providing an incorrect tax identification number, such as a Social Security number. If the IRS does not receive a correct tax identification number from the taxpayer, or believes that the taxpayer is under-reporting income. the IRS will calculate the backup withholding amount by applying a flat 28% backup withholding rate to income received from interest payments, dividends, patronage dividends, rents, profits, and other gains, commissions and other payments received as a contractor, payments by brokers, royalty payments, and certain other payments as defined by IRS Publication 505. Backup withholding disputes are generally resolved by providing the proper information to the IRS, or proving that income reporting is appropriate.

Personal Time, Fatigue and Delay allowances

Normal fatigue prevents all employees, not just those with disabilities, from producing at their most rapid pace throughout the workday. In addition, breaks, cleanup time, and delay time while materials are being restocked or the finished products are removed all reduce the amount a worker can produce. Employers must take this nonproductive time into consideration when determining piece rates used to compute special minimum wages by including what is known as a Personal Time, Fatigue, and Delay (PF&D) Factor. Federal regulations state that when determining piece rates, "appropriate time shall be allowed for personal time, fatigue, and unavoidable delays." Generally, not less than 15% allowances (9 - 10 minutes per hour) shall be used in conducting time studies."

The Personal Time, Fatigue & Disability (PF&D) allowance can be properly incorporated when determining the piece rates to be paid workers with disabilities in several different ways. The simplest method is to conduct time studies of the standard setters (workers who do not have disabilities for the work performed) for 25 minutes, and then multiply the number of completed units by 2. Averaging those results will yield the standard - the number of units that an experienced worker without disabilities would be expected to produce in an hour with a properly computed 10-minute PF&D. The piece rate is then obtained by dividing the hourly prevailing wage rate for the work by the standard. For a 9-minute PF&D, the standard setters would be timed for 25½ minutes.

Suppose that an employer must establish a piece rate to determine the wages due workers with disabilities paid special minimum wages who are employed to produce a specific product requiring hand assembly. The employer has already conducted a survey and determined that the prevailing wage rate for that work in the vicinity is $8 an hour. By conducting time studies of three experienced workers who do not have disabilities for the work being performed for 25 minutes and averaging the number of completed units produced, the employer determined that the average number of units produced in 25 minutes was 40. Therefore, the standard for this job, using a 10-minute PF&D, is 80 units. The employer would then divide the prevailing wage rate ($8) by the standard (80 units) to determine a piece rate of $0.10.

Federal Tax Deposits

Federal Tax Deposits (FTDs) for Form 941 are made up of withholding taxes or trust funds (income tax and Federal Insurance Contributions Act (FICA) taxes, which are Social Security and Medicare held in trust), that are actually part of the employee's wages, along with the employer's matching half of FICA. FTDs for Form 940 are taxes paid by the employer to provide for unemployment compensation to workers who have lost their jobs. Only the employer pays FUTA tax; it is not deducted from the employee's wages. These taxes need to be paid as they become due in order to avoid penalties. If you have a deposit requirement, you may be able to choose one of two deposit methods: Electronic Federal Tax Payment System (EFTPS) or using the FTD coupons (Form 8109-B) if you are not using, or required to use, the EFTPS.

Employers may have two separate employment tax deposits: 1) employers filing Form 941, Employer's Quarterly Federal Tax Return, with $2,500 or more tax due per quarter, or 2) employers filing Form 940, Employer's Annual Federal Unemployment Tax Return (FUTA), with over $500 tax due per quarter. Employers with a deposit requirement for Form 940, make the deposit by the last day of the first month after the quarter ends. If an employer has a deposit requirement for Form 941, there are two ways to remember: A) make a deposit the same day you pay your employees, or B) make the deposit before the Form 941 Deposit Due Date. Monthly Schedule Depositors should deposit taxes from all of their paydays in a month by the 15th of the next month, even if they pay wages every week.

Payroll Process and Supporting Systems and Administration

Employee master file

A master file of employee data is typically created for purposes of compliance with federal regulations and should contain the following data:

EMPLOYEE		
• Name • Address • Sex	• Birthdate • Work Location • SSN	• Employee # • Classification • State Location
EMPLOYMENT / WAGE-HOUR		
• Hire date • Termination date • Payment date • Exempt/Nonexempt	• Hourly rate • Adds/Deducts • Shift diff. • Pay Frequency	• Hours per day • Hours per week • Workweek • Straight/Overtime
TAX AND PAYROLL		
• Allowances • Additional Withholding	• Filing Status • Exemption Status	
PER PERIOD AND CALENDAR YEAR		
• Wages subject to income tax • Social Security WH • Medicare tax WH • Wages subject to SS, Medicare tax	• Total Compensation • Total income tax withheld • Total wages subject to SS, Medicare tax	• State unemployment • State disability • Taxes paid by employer but not deducted from wages

Self-service payroll applications

As the name implies, Shared Services represents the consolidation or centralization of services which are common to, or shared by, multiple entities or multiple organizations within an entity. In addition to Payroll, such administrative type services as Human Resources, Compensation, Accounts Payable and Accounts Receivable are often organized as a shared service. The objective of such an organization is to improve the level of service provided to the customers who are typically the at-large employees of an entity. Service is improved by standardizing and simplifying processes, employing best practices and adopting rigorous training regimen for the service center employees. The intent is to offer a sort of "one-stop shopping" for the customers of the shared service center. For the sponsoring employer, the shared service center is intended to create process and labor efficiencies which are translated into lower or more rational costs. The typical types of services provided via self-service payroll applications are as follows:

- Personal data updates such as changes to address, telephone, marital and dependent status.
- Secured access to earnings history including payroll check stubs and Forms W-2.

- Secured access to benefits information such as available and used vacation and sick time.
- Requests for error corrections or replacement of paychecks.
- Access to forms, instructions and policies and procedures.
- Timekeeping functions such as start and stop time registration and time reporting.

System data edits

System edits in the context of an automated payroll system represent a type of alert system whereby anomalies create messages to system administrators to check for possible malfunctions. Tolerance ranges can be defined in order to flag process results that are beyond normal expectations. For example, a pay week in which the hours worked are greater than say, 50, could create an alert requiring action by an operator or manager. Some of the more commonly used system edits are as follows:
- Payments to an employee with a pending termination.
- Payments to new employees requiring verification.
- Lack of payment to an active employee.
- Zero or negative net pay or deductions.
- Earnings beyond a threshold or expected range amount.

Integrating or interfacing the payroll system with other automated systems

An integrated system, whether payroll or some other application, generally refers to a system design that allows multiple applications to use common transactional and master data. The objective is to ensure accuracy by using a single source of data and improve efficiency by eliminating the necessity of multiple data entry points. A system that is interfaced (to another system) is one in which data is transmitted between the systems but each retains its own transactional and master data. In the case of payroll, an integrated system would be one in which payroll and, say, human resources are separate applications within a single system. A single source exists for all employee personal, wage and tax data that can be used by each of the payroll and human resources applications. Changes made by one group are instantly available to the other. The most common system that is typically integrated with a payroll system is Human Resources. Other systems that could be integrated but are more commonly interfaced are as follows:
- General Ledger – posting of all payroll accounting data.
- Accounts Payable – payment of deduction payments.
- Treasury – funding information for payroll and tax deposits and detailed employee payment information for bank reconciliations.
- Time and Attendance – arrival and departure, hours worked.
- Direct Deposit/Paycards – electronic files for transmission to the ACH.
- Labor Cost – distribution of hours worked by cost centers.

The most common reason for integrating a payroll and human resource (including employee benefits) system is because both systems use the same source of master data: employee information. Such information need only be maintained once at a single point in order to be available to both systems. Transactions which are processed in one system, such as the accrual of vacation time in human resources, are available to the other system, such as the payment of the accrued vacation time in payroll. The use of a single source also facilitates the maintenance of the security and confidentiality of the data.

Batch and hash totals

Batching is a process used in some systems whereby input data is sorted into smaller groups in order to facilitate input and output control. Hash totals represent control figures that facilitate the verification of inputs and outputs. The objective is to ensure that all data that was intended to be processed by the system was actually so processed. However, the control that is provided only relates to the quantity of data and not to the accuracy.

Correction
Where errors are detected, either from the batch process and hash totals or from other sources, procedural controls must be in place with which to manage the correction process. The procedures should be sufficient to enable the operator to not only determine the error but also the root cause and the proper method of correction, either by reversal and reentry or a single correcting entry.

Real-time processing vs. batch processing

The real-time processing of data refers to a system in which the database is continually updated as transactions are processed through the system. In contrast, the batch processing of data involves temporarily storing the processed data throughout a period of time, such as a business day, and then updating the database with all transactions at the end of the period (overnight, prior to the next business day). As a result, queries of the data in a batch system will return results that do not reflect the most current transactions. Real-time data queries will return results that were often updated only minutes or seconds before.

Accumulator totals

Wage and tax information of employees and employers is subject to significant levels of regulation by both federal and state government. Much of the regulation requires reporting via the filing of returns and the time period to be reported varies depending upon the regulatory entity and the type of payment. As a result, a payroll system must provide accumulated totals for various time periods in order to enable regulatory compliance. Additionally, some taxes are applicable only to partial amounts of the earnings of an employee. For example, unemployment tax is applicable only to the first $7,000 in earnings and social security tax cannot be applied to income greater than $118,500 (for 2016).

Testing during implementation project

The implementation of any software project including payroll is always preceded by a testing phase to ensure that the system functions as per design. The testing is typically conducted in phases beginning with what is termed unit testing. A unit test is designed to verify the functional operation of a specific component within the overall system. For example, a payroll system unit test might consist of checking each deduction or verifying the calculation of wages to be paid. The step which follows unit testing is often described as a system test, in which the functional operation of the entire system (end-to-end) is verified. For example, a payroll system test might consist of processing an entire payroll cycle, beginning with time entry and ending with payments and tax deposits. The overall objective of the testing phase is to ensure that the software will produce the desired results one the system is implemented and the data becomes "live."

<u>Unit testing</u>
Parallel testing of new payroll software is a form of system testing whereby the end-to-end processing of transactions is tested prior to the formal implementation with live data. Therefore, in order to be appropriately prepared to test an entire system, each of the major components of the system must first be individually tested, a process that is called unit testing. An end-to-end system test must always take place before formal implementation but it is not always conducted as a parallel test. Rather than test a new system in parallel with the operation of the system to be replaced (i.e. running both systems simultaneously), companies often choose to avoid the time and cost by advancing directly to the implementation phase after the system test. In theory, the higher risk is offset by the lower cost and shorter timing.

Security measures in a payroll system

Security measures in a payroll system as part of the system of internal control include the following:
- Segregation of job duties – to ensure that a single employee cannot create inappropriate transactions.
- Rotation of job assignments – to ensure process standardization and employee cross-training, as well as discouraging inappropriate behavior by long-ensconced employees.
- Paychecks are delivered only to employees
- Physical payouts – employees are required to provide identification to receive delivery of paychecks, to prevent so-called ghost employees.
- Background checks – of payroll employees to ensure high ethical standards.

Functionality of a computer system

As the word implies, functionality refers to the functions of a system that can be performed or are available to be performed. In the case of payroll software, the common functionality includes the following:
- Pay processing – calculating and paying wages, withholding and accounting for deductions, creating records of all activity.
- Payroll Reporting – providing reports and analytics.
- Check Printing – printing checks and earnings statements and providing bank reconciliation reporting.
- Direct Deposit/Paycards – creating electronic files with which to transmit information to the ACH.
- Retirement plan reporting – calculation and reporting earnings information for retirement plan.
- Garnishment processing – calculation and reporting of deductions subject to income and legal requirements.

Various payroll operating and government reports

Payroll operating reports are important for facilitating management control over the labor costs of an organization. Such reports are designed to provide managers with both the static and analytic data with which to understand labor costs and implement adjustments as necessary. Reporting also supports the administration of benefit programs such as pensions and 401(k) plans. Reports designed to provide regulatory required data facilitate the ability of an organization to remain in compliance with tax and labor regulations. Examples of such reporting include quarterly earnings and withholding for Form 941 filings as well as annual earnings and withholding for Form 944 and Form W-2 filings.

Backing up computer files

A good backup strategy should be planned carefully. Points to consider include:
- Creating backups according to a fixed time cycle (daily, weekly, etc.) can improve data recovery reliability.
- Automated backup can help reduce human error.
- Making multiple copies of the backup can increase potential for data recovery in the event of a disaster.
- Weigh using established backup format standards against new standards. Established standards are usually safer for recovery, but new standards are generally faster and more powerful.
- Data compression techniques may be advisable if media space is an issue, but compression requires special software and slows information retrieval. .

Backups are important both for security and for disaster recovery. Natural disasters, accidents, terrorism, hack attacks, viruses, etc. pose danger to the physical facilities, to the hardware and software computer resources, and to the digitized files themselves. A good backup and disaster recovery plan includes a provision for rotational backups (a so-called grandfather-father-son scheme) with multiple copies of backups to be stored at multiple remote locations. Having the most recent backup available at an alternate secure location where it can be readily accessed can significantly reduce company downtime in case of a disaster or computer mishap

Utility of backups
Loss of computer information can mean disaster for the entity. The term "backups" is computer terminology used to describe the process or results of copying digitized information, (file structures, user files, system files, etc.) to another storage device or media in order to ensure information is available in case original information is damaged or destroyed. This differs from archiving, in which original information is intentionally moved from the original storage device or media to make room for more current information while providing access to the archived information when needed. In both cases, a good disaster recovery plan includes a requirement for multiple copies to be stored in multiple secure, offsite locations.

Backup media types
Once, tape was considered the most viable storage medium for backing up large amounts of digitized information. Now, large capacity magnetic tape, hard disk storage, and optical disk WORM (Write Once, Read Many times) media such as CD-R and DVD-R are all viable backup options, particularly when used with newer file compression techniques. The increasing availability and use of broadband access makes network and remote backup, or online backup, a more viable option.

<u>Checksums</u>
Many backup programs utilize checksums or hashes. This allows data integrity to be verified without reference to the original file; if the file as stored on the backup medium has the same checksum as the saved value, then it is probable that data integrity has been maintained in the copy. Some backup programs can use checksums to reduce the need for redundant copies of files, and thereby improve backup speed. This is particularly useful when backing up multiple workstations over a network, since each workstation may contain its own copy of the same file; if the backup software detects several copies of a file having the same size, date stamp, and checksum, it can backup one copy of the data and include metadata listing all network locations where copies of this file were found.

Firewall

A firewall helps to protect computer resources from unauthorized access. The firewall creates a virtual wall that separates trusted and untrusted environments by controlling and regulating the traffic through data ports between these two environments. This helps protect the trusted environment from harmful activity such as intrusion attacks. Firewalls are available as both hardware and software, or as a combination of both.

Disaster recovery plan

A well-designed backup plan should balance cost and effectiveness. Some issues that should be considered include the amount of downtime that is acceptable; the cost of downtime; the required speed of recovery; and the amount of acceptable data loss. What is considered acceptable can vary widely, depending on the industry, the particular business and system, and the particular situation. For example, a construction contractor may be able to tolerate more downtime than an e-commerce site taking orders 24 hours a day, but the construction contractor may require less downtime potential on the day of the payroll run.

An office disaster recovery plan should prioritize data needs. Not all data is created equal, and certain needs will require more current information to be readily available in case of a disaster. For instance, accounting data and personnel records are more important to disaster recovery than operational statistics and EPA reports. Other factors, such as the form of media (paper versus digital) may also deserve consideration. As a final result, a well-planned disaster recovery plan should be easy to understand and follow, and should provide for responsibility levels, regular maintenance schedules, and a prioritized approach to getting the company back up and running.

<u>System recovery speed</u>
System recovery speed requirements are closely related to the amount of uptime required, but may also depend on the type of problem involved. Customers, vendors, and lenders may be understanding in the case of a manmade or natural disaster, but less so in the case of a disk crash or a corrupted data file. A good disaster recovery plan should minimize downtime in such cases.

<u>Acceptable data loss</u>
There is an inverse relationship between the amount of data you can afford to lose and the requirements of your backup and disaster recovery plan. The degree of inverse correlation may vary according to industry, company, and situation. A large bank, for instance, probably can't afford to lose even one transaction. In other cases, the business may be able to follow

the paper trail to recapture activity for a limited period of time. Often, cost is a primary factor in determining the degree of risk of potential data loss the business is willing to assume.

Clear lines of duties

Clear lines of responsibility and duties are essential to any disaster recovery plan. Business continuity depends on it. Payrolls must be processed. Vendors must be paid. Employees must be notified to return to work. Depending on the situation, media contacts may require activation. Accounts receivable must be collected. Business life must go on. Moving forward is difficult, however, if managers and employees do not understand their roles in the recovery process. Just as with school fire drills, periodic disaster recovery drills may be advisable so that everyone knows what they are supposed to do – and so they will respond in an efficient, organized fashion if disaster strikes.

Setting priorities

Priorities should be set when a disaster recovery/business continuity plan is developed. A disaster recovery plan that protects every document or business process is probably not cost-effective. A good disaster recovery plan should discern between the business information that is absolutely critical to business survival and the business information that is not. Even then, the degree of business recovery difficulty can vary for given functions; business continuity should be the main focus. For instance, a business can request that their banking institution use the same payroll amount as that of the previous pay period to cover a disaster-affected period's payroll. Overpayments and underpayments can be handled later.

Selection of disaster recovery center

Several important factors should be considered when selecting a disaster recovery services provider, among them:

- Location. Too close and the provider could be affected by the disaster. Too remote and needed resources may not be readily available.
- Stability. A financially insolvent firm may not be there to help you when disaster strikes.
- Service model. Are the facilities and services shared or dedicated?
- Other customers. The greater the number of customers using the facilities (particularly from the same geographic locale), the more stress may be placed on provider resources after a disaster.
- Physical and logical security. Access to your information should be restricted and tightly controlled.

System compatibility: Since the disaster recovery center will potentially be used as a base of operations immediately after a disaster, the disaster recovery computer system must be compatible with your computer system. You should be able to perform necessary recovery operations without reconfiguring your system. Recovery computer system expandability can also be a factor as your needs change. The number and quality of telephone lines into the disaster recovery facility, and the level and availability of business-class broadband communications service should be reviewed based on your requirements. Representatives from your organization should be responsible for ensuring continued compatibility between computer systems.

Disaster notification and response: Your recovery center should be available 24 hours a day. Disaster center response time requirements vary depending upon the business situation. A four hour response time may be considered reasonable. Authorized personnel should be required to identify themselves using a prearranged codeword or other method when notifying the disaster recovery facility to initiate disaster recovery procedures.

Steps taken after disaster
The computer hardware and media that holds the data should first be located. If you are working with emergency or other personnel, let them know that the computer and media you are looking for contain confidential information. Once the items are located, remove them from the disaster site as quickly as is possible. Make a concentrated effort to do as little additional damage as possible. After the items have been moved to as secure a place as possible, inspect them to determine what type of damage has taken place. In many cases, it is likely that some part of the computer or media have been physically destroyed or harmed. A good disaster recovery plan should include a listing of resources already developed who provide specialized data recovery services if needed.

Disaster recovery vs. planning for business continuity

Disaster recovery is the process of resuming business after a sudden event disrupts normal business operations. The event may be large (tornado) or small (computer virus). "Business continuity planning" is a more comprehensive approach to business survival, and includes not only disaster planning but also provisions for changes in key personnel or ownership, supply chain disruptions, etc.

Choosing and buying payroll software

Initial steps in buying computer payroll software include:
- determine how much of the payroll process will be performed in-house
- determine who will install and maintain the software
- determine the skill level of entity personnel who will use the software
- determine the level of software training and support needed versus that available
- determine the level of additional hardware and software investment necessary to facilitate the new payroll software
- determine the cost of each project component, the total project cost, and the financial resources available for the purchase – then align costs with resources.

Cost and benefit considerations
A number of questions are involved and factors should be considered before implementing software systems. Analysis of costs and benefits is one of several approaches that can be used to determine the value a particular payroll software system provides to the organization. For such an analysis, the following formula can be used:
Return = Benefits – Costs
Calculating the return on investment will require you to quantify the costs of implementing the payroll software versus the benefits it provides.

Evaluating whether to outsource payroll

Depending on the needs of the particular business, outsourcing the payroll processing function can result in a significant reduction in payroll department workload and required level of inhouse payroll expertise. The business entity should consider and look for the level of service that meets its needs. In some cases, the total payroll function can be easily outsourced. Other entities may find that only part of the payroll function can be outsourced – usually this relates to printing payroll checks ; accounting for and remitting payroll taxes; and reporting to the employee (paystub and W-2), the appropriate governmental entity (federal Forms 941 and 944, for instance), the employer, and others as required. In yet other cases, the business may find that its peculiar needs or preferences cannot or should not be outsourced.

Automated labor management software

Automated labor management applications assist with forecasting, scheduling, reporting, and numerous other functions. Point of service-integrated applications, PC-based applications and Web-based applications can all be used for labor scheduling. Each of these approaches works to streamline processes related to the human resources function and enhance workforce controls. Such systems reduce or eliminate manual effort and provide real-time data for management review and decision making.

Overtime monitoring
Businesses must consider overtime in any plan to address labor costs. Overtime may be unavoidable, but labor management software helps restrict overtime to only that which is "pre-approved". The labor management software notifies management as an employee's work hours approach the overtime threshold and requires managerial approval before counting any hours in excess of the threshold.

Controlling lost time
Labor management systems control early sign-ins and late sign-outs by refusing to count time worked unless it is within the employee's authorized schedule. Payment outside these parameters requires managerial/supervisory authorization. Both automated control and an override procedure are thereby provided.

Evaluation of costs in implementing software systems

When evaluating the costs of a new software system, businesses must consider total project costs, not just those related to the cost of the software itself. System implementation can be extremely expensive. Among the factors to consider: 1) consulting fees for outside services and expertise (such as from the Value Added Reseller); 2) requirements analysis, including documentation of practices and requirements necessary to implement the system; 3) custom software programming, if the out-of-the-box software product does not adequately meet the entity's needs; and 4) software installation and deployment costs throughout the organization.

Modern time and attendance software systems

Today's time and attendance systems fall into three major categories based on how they collect information: time clock-oriented, manager or time keeper-oriented and employee-oriented. With clock-oriented systems, little or no support is present in the software for employees or managers to report time directly through a computer. Those oriented to manager or time keeper are designed to "partially" automate the time entry process. Employees record and/or report time through a traditional punch clock or sign-in sheet. The sign-in sheets are then collected and passed to a manager or "time keeper" who is responsible for entering the information into the time and attendance system. Employee-oriented systems are designed for "white collar" environments; here, employees report their own time through a computer.

Evolution of time recording software

The very first computerized timekeeping systems were software designed to collect and store attendance information downloaded from a time clock. This type of system replaced the older punch clocks found at many work places, and would capture the date and time when the employee came to work and left the job. In recent years, the "direct time reporting" method has gained popularity. This method requires the employee to log into the time sheet system and manually enter his or her attendance information.

Providing appropriate payroll system back-up procedures

Providing for a back-up of payroll system data ensures that key data is not lost in the event of software or hardware failures, power losses or major catastrophic events. Data should be copied at regular intervals to minimize the amount of restoration required in the event of an incident. The interval period will depend upon the volume and nature of transactional activity; a high volume environment may require a back-up multiple times during a business day whereas comparatively low volume environments may need a back-up only daily or even weekly.

Effective system documentation manual

An effective payroll operations manual should include, at minimum, the following functional topics:
- Event schedules (payroll periods, pay dates, deposit dates, etc.)
- Time entry
- Adjustment and corrections entry
- Calculation of checks
- Earnings history
- Production cycle (from time entry to payment)
- Taxes and deposit procedures
- Management of employee data base
- Reporting

Payroll Administration and Management

Assessing skills and abilities of payroll staff applicants

Where specific knowledge and skills are required of an applicant, open ended questions are an effective method for determination. Rather than asking if an applicant is familiar with say, SOX compliance, the applicant might be asked to explain the requirements of SOX. Additional determination can be obtained using a service from the American Payroll Association (APA) which is called Knowledge Assessment Calculator (KAC) in which the applicant provides answers to 50 questions and a knowledge assessment is immediately provided to the manager.

Performance evaluations

Performance evaluations are used as a formal, documented method of providing feedback to employees, assessing performance and identifying required improvements. Specific reasons include the following:
- To identify high and low achievers.
- To substantiate salary differentials and increases.
- To identify future promotion candidates.
- To support training requirements or disciplinary actions.
- To encourage growth and development.
- To provide documentation for legal compliance.

The general components of a performance evaluation system that can be expected to be effective include the following:
- Objective goals, objectives and performance assessment criteria.
- Training for managers responsible for conducting evaluations.
- Written guidelines for the proper conduct of evaluations.
- Employee feedback is provided for.
- Procedures are reasonable in terms of actions and timing.

Benchmarking

Benchmarking is the process of gathering best practice data from outside sources, often from peers and/or competitors with which to develop comparisons to the internal practices of a company. The objective is to establish a performance standard, using a measure such as a key performance indicator (KPI) in order to drive process improvements. In a customer service context, benchmarks can be used with respect to response times and solution accuracy. For example, in a payroll context, assume that the calculation process for paychecks yields an accuracy ratio (KPI) of 97.6%. In order to assess this performance, a benchmark can be obtained for comparison. If the benchmark is, say 99.8%, then it is clear that there is room for improvement.

Training for payroll employees

The common types of training available for payroll employees are as follows:
- Classroom training – offered by service providers, educational institutions and software companies; the American Payroll Association (APA) also offers web-based tutorials.
- Feedback – corrective behavior suggested by a manager can function as an effective training tool, assuming the context is educational and not punitive.
- Coaching – represents feedback more formally provided, usually as the result of an observance session.
- Demonstration – presentation of information by a subject matter expert.
- Goal Establishment – the establishment of mutually agreeable goals (between the manager and the employee).

Job interview technique

The actual recruiting process should begin with an assessment of the current job description with the objective of ascertaining accuracy and validity. From the revised job description, a list of questions to be asked of all candidates can be developed. It is important that all candidates be asked most, if not all of the same questions so as to prevent any unintentional bias. The interviewer should be seeking to determine the presence (or lack thereof) of the technical and performance skills that were identified in the revised job descriptions. An effective method of questioning an applicant is to use open-ended questions (i.e. questions that cannot be answered with a single word such as yes or no). An applicant that is asked to describe or explain a certain technique or process will present two opportunities for assessment: a demonstration of the thinking process and communicative abilities, as well as specific knowledge of the information requested.

Job description information

The principal types of information that are often included in a job description are as follows:
- Specific responsibilities and activities required to be performed in the job.
- Educational requirements in order to perform the activities of the job.
- Prerequisite knowledge and skills.
- Training opportunities (for a new employee).
- Level of required supervision, both of incumbent and subordinates.
- Interaction and communication amongst the organization.

Positive feedback

If managers want employees to repeat successes, they must point them out so that employees understand what they did right. This is the essence of positive feedback. Managers should also remember when taking corrective action that criticism should be focused on the issue and not the person. Negative feedback should focus on one or two points (and not become a laundry list of frustrations), and it should be ended, where possible, with a positive note concerning something the employee did right. The use of positive feedback has been proven to be an effective tool for motivating employees and for creating a positive working environment.

Clarity in project management

Project managers must be clear in defining project goals to ensure that all project workers understand their assignments and their roles within the project. Often, defining project goals entails dissecting goals into individual objectives and assigned tasks; and then tracking project progress and measuring progress against project standards (using Gantt and Pert charts, and other tools).

Delegation

Delegation helps the manager, the employee, and the organization. The manager is freed to devote time to areas not otherwise delegated. Employees are allowed to use and develop their skills and knowledge. In so doing, employees learn to apply their skills and knowledge to new situations and make good decisions with minimal guidance. The company gains through increased productivity and improved work climate. As employees grow, it is important to grant authority commensurate with the delegated responsibility. Failure to do so can result in employee frustration and damage the work climate.

Information flow
Successful delegation requires that decision-makers (your staff) have full and access to relevant information as quickly as possible. This necessitates a free flow of information via regular exchanges between you and your staff so that each person is aware of what the others are doing. Briefings by you should include the information which you have received in your role as manager that your staff will need to know in order to perform delegated tasks. Without such free flow of information, employees may become frustrated because they are unable to adequately perform the delegated tasks.

Control
Rather than losing control through delegation of tasks, managers may find they actually gain control. Employees will learn to perform tasks the way the manager prefers, and effectively become extensions of the manager. The end result is that the manager's control may be exerted in multiple places simultaneously.

Impact of manager's behavior

A manager's attitude can dramatically impact the other members of the team. Managers who always find fault will never be pleased, and the other members of the team will stop trying to please them. A manager who frowns on risk-taking and independent decision making will soon find no one wants to risk making independent decisions. The work climate will suffer, and the manager will find that the team's effectiveness is limited.

Motivating subordinates

Managers should remember certain key points concerning motivating employees. First, negative reinforcement techniques (using the stick without the carrot) have limited success at best, and do not work over the long term. Second, money ceases to be a prime motivator at some point. Once employees deem compensation to be fair, they seek other motivators such as challenge, opportunity for advancement, and a positive work environment that includes recognition for achievement. These become the tools successful managers can use to motivate employees, increase productivity and effectiveness, and gain personal recognition as an effective leader.

<u>Recognition</u>
Recognition motivates. It tells employees what they did right last time so they can repeat the experience. It tells them someone cares how well they perform on the job. It tells them someone appreciates when they take initiative and make good decisions. Recognition improves employee morale and increases the manager's effectiveness as a leader.

<u>Responsibility</u>
Responsibility is one of the most lasting motivators, but responsibility must eventually be accompanied by commensurate authority to ward off potential frustration. This is a delicate balance; successful assignment of responsibility can promote employee growth and boost morale, but granting of commensurate authority should done carefully to ensure the employee has grown sufficiently to successfully exercise it and make good decisions. If done properly, employee morale, work climate, and team productivity will benefit

Level of interest in assigned tasks

Employee performance can suffer when assigned tasks lack challenge or interest. Managers can improve effectiveness and productivity by ensuring that task assignments for each employee contain some measure of challenge and potential reward.

Manager roles

The manager has three major roles: that of planner, provider and protector. As planner, the manager must plan effectively, selecting the optimal plan for the team and implementing it. As provider, the Manager has access to, and provides, resources the team needs while exercising authority for the benefit of the team. As protector, the manager guards the team against problems and distractions that can deflect the work-force from the important issues.

Management theories

<u>Contingency theory</u>
Contingency theory asserts that managers must take into account all aspects of the current situation and act on the key aspects of that situation. Their decision, in other words, depends on consideration of the key aspects of the each situation. For example, someone leading troops into a protracted battle may conclude that an autocratic style is best while someone leading a hospital or university may choose a more participative and facilitative leadership style.

<u>Chaos theory</u>
Chaos theory asserts that events in business (or in life) are rarely controlled. Many chaos theorists suggest that systems naturally become more complex over time, and as they do so, these systems become more volatile and must expend more energy to maintain their complexity. This in turn causes them to seek more structure to maintain stability. The trend continues until the system splits, combines with another complex system, or disintegrates.

Systems theory

In management, the systems theory has had a significant effect on understanding organizations. A system is a collection of parts assembled to accomplish an overall goal. A change in the composition changes the nature of the system as well. A system can be viewed as having inputs, processes, outputs and outcomes. Systems theory provides a new perspective for managers to interpret patterns and events in the workplace. Managers recognize both the various parts of the organization and the interrelations of those parts. This integration represents a major development in management science.

Weber's bureaucratic management theory

Sociologist Max Weber, the father of bureaucratic management, developed a hierarchical system in which individuals were granted a series of primary occupations and responsibilities within an office. A systematic division of labor pursued organizational goals and objectives and made each lower office accountable to the next higher one. People were chosen for their position based on their qualifications. Their responsibilities were limited to the primary occupations or classifications assigned to them when they were hired. Promotions rewarded seniority, achievement or both. Under Weber's plan, promotions were unaffected by office politics, and workers were expected to separate personal affairs from business responsibilities.

Scientific management theory

Frederick Taylor developed what became known as the "scientific management theory," advocating careful specification and measurement of all organizational tasks. Under this theory, tasks were standardized as much as possible and workers were rewarded and punished. Assembly lines and other mechanistic, routine activities seemed well suited to this approach. The popularity of the scientific management theory has waned since about 1940.

Management skills

Change management

Change is a common occurrence in business today; because of this, it is important that you possess strong change management skills if you want your business to be a success. Change management skills include leadership development (to get people to believe in you), marketing and sales abilities (to promote your case for change), and communication skills (to help build support for the decision to change). It will also help if you know a little about the stages people go through psychologically when they are dealing with change so that you are able to tell if you have managed a successful transition or if there are additional problems that you need to address.

Building your ability as a leader is the first step in the change management process. Once employees believe in you and trust what you're doing, you can then begin your campaign for change. Your campaign should target the different groups within your business and outline the reasons why change is necessary for each. For instance, the board of directors will want to know what the long-term effects of the change will be. Similarly, your employees will want to know how they will be personally effected by the changes you are proposing. Once a change occurs, it is very important to communicate on a regular basis with all affected. Let your employees know what is happening.

The first thing you will want to focus on in change management is your leadership ability. Companies continue to make the mistake of focusing too much on business processes and not enough on good, strong examples of leadership. To be an effective leader in the change management process, it helps if you:

- Set an example. As the top person in your business, others look to you for direction not only in terms of business needs, but also related to behavior, ethics, and standards. If you want others in your business to change, you must set an example for them to follow.
- Eliminate perks. Perks suggest division and hierarchical thought processes. By eliminating or reducing your own perks, you show your desire to level the playing field.
- Be genuine. As a leader of change, it is important to be as real and honest as possible in your interactions with others.

Budgeting

Budgeting, as a management skill, is a useful tool in forecasting potential shortfalls in operations, and identifying potentially problematic areas of spending. It also facilitates communication between managers and subordinates, while keeping them on the same page or working toward the same goal. Budgeting provides awareness to all who are involved in the process, and may lead to more cooperation between departments and individuals. Budgeting also assists in more efficient uses of company resources, as employees and managers become more aware of the limitations and needs of the company. When the budget is prepared by a committee of individuals involved from different departments, it engages the business as a whole and the dangers of planning from a narrow point of view can be avoided. For budgeting to be effective as a management skill, it must be followed and compared throughout the year with actual results of running the business.

Business planning

Business planning is the process of charting a long-term course for a business to take. By writing a business plan, employers try to determine what obstacles and opportunities lie ahead and plan for the best courses of action to take advantage of the opportunities and overcome the obstacles. As part of the plan, the employer must consider the present state of the business and the industry, develop goals to be achieved, plot the best course to meeting those goals, and then determine if the cost to achieve those goals does not exceed the required rate of return on the venture. Internal audits, budgeting sessions, and plan assessments are all vital parts of the business planning process. Having a well-prepared and thoroughly vetted business plan will only assist the business owner if the owner follows the plan. Employers have many resources of which to take advantage when writing a business plan. Many books and magazines address the issue, and the government has published web pages to assist in the writing of effective business plans.

Time management techniques

There are numerous methods for effective time management, but among the most widely recognized and accepted as effective are The Pomodoro Technique, the 18 Minutes technique, the COPE technique, and the ABC and Pareto Analyses combination technique. The Pomodoro Technique hypothesizes that the human mind focuses optimally for only 25 minutes at a time, and that a person should take a five minute break every 25 minutes, with a longer break after the fourth 25 minute period. The 18 Minutes Technique suggests taking 18 minutes of reflection each day to help plan your day: five minutes in the morning to determine the important tasks ahead, a minute each hour to reflect on the productivity of that hour, and five minutes at the end of the day to determine how productive the day was. The COPE method advises employees to analyze how their day is spent by keeping a log of activities, and then eliminating time wasters. The ABC/Pareto Combo method encourages employees to determine which tasks are important, which are urgent, and which are neither, and accomplish the urgent/important tasks first.

Management by objectives

Peter Drucker is credited with popularizing the term "Management by Objectives." The term describes a process of agreeing upon objectives within an organization so that management and employees buy in to the objectives and understand what they are. MBO requires a rather precise written description of objectives and time lines for monitoring progress and achievement. The process requires agreement between the manager and the employee as to employee achievement goals, and also requires that the employee accept and buy into the objectives, otherwise commitment will be lacking.

Variation in reaching phases of change

It is important to note that people in your organizations will proceed through the different phases of change at different rates of speed. One person may require two months to reach Phase 6 while another may require twelve. To make things even more complex, the cycle of change is not linear. In other words, a person does not necessarily complete Phase 1 through 6 in order. It is much more common for people to jump around. One person may go from Phase 4 to Phase 5 and then back to Phase 2 again; that is why there is no easy way to determine how long a change will take to implement. However, by using good leadership skills, you increase your chances of managing the change as effectively as possible.

Rewarding customer service workers

Recognizing excellence in customer service work often leads to better performance of customer service workers. There are three basic types of recognition that an employee might find inspiring to perform at the next level. Peer recognition involves collecting positive feedback from the employee's peers and acknowledging the feedback in a public or private setting, but it is typically more effective in a public setting. Leadership recognition should be given in public settings. When given in public settings, the employee has the additional benefit of being seen as a leader in his or her department. Customer recognition comes from the customer and expresses that the customer service professional assisted in an excellent or outstanding way. Since the customer generally informs the supervisor of the customer service professional of his or her good experience, it is up to the supervisor to let the employee know. For maximum effect on the employee's self-esteem, it is best to acknowledge him or her in public.

Dealing with frustration in communication

It is important as a leader to recognize inconvenience or frustration and offer solutions, particularly if you need someone else's cooperation or your activities will affect them. Don't offer advice unless asked. Look for common ground rather than focusing only on differences. Remember that change is stressful for most people, particularly if your activities affect them in a way that they cannot control.

Good communication skills

Excellent communication skills are essential for good performance management. They are important competencies used in the entire performance management process, from planning and communicating work expectations to recognizing employees for their successful achievements. To communicate effectively with employees, performance managers must:

- establish strong working relationships with employees
- promote easy access to information and feedback
- promote employee involvement in planning and development activities
- recognize and praise top performers.

It must be remembered that establishing an effective working relationship with each employee takes time and effort. The best managers make certain each employee feels connected and valued. Competent managers individualize their efforts to communicate with employees, recognize employees' strengths, and support their development.

Improving listening skills

Good listening often means asking good questions and then paying close attention to the answer. When someone makes prickly comments or complaints, it is often out of concern or fear. By asking the right questions and paying attention to not only what is answered but how questions are answered, one can get to the bottom of someone's real concern or agenda.

Audits

Internal control system

The internal control system of a company exists for the purpose of ensuring that the financial records are accurate and timely presented and that the assets are subject to levels of security sufficient for preservation of value. Such a system will consist of a series of checks and balances with which to ensure that transactions are properly posted and property is properly controlled. Internal control is a key component of an audit, whether required for internal purposes or required for regulatory compliance such as with the Sarbanes-Oxley (SOX) Act.

Segregating job duties

The segregation of job duties is a component of an internal control system that is intended to minimize the opportunity for a single employee to control an end-to-end process and thereby commit a fraud or embezzlement of funds. Examples of segregated job duties include the following:
- The reconcilement of payroll related general ledger and bank accounts is performed by the accounting department, not by the payroll department.
- Managers are provided employee lists with which to check against a list of employees who receive paychecks.
- Payroll check stock and undistributed paychecks are maintained out of the control of the payroll department.
- Unclaimed wages and escheatment is controlled by the accounting department and not the payroll department.
- Employee master file data is maintained by the human resources department, not the payroll department.

Following a payroll distribution process

As a fraud prevention measure, paychecks should be distributed directly and only to the employee. The intent is to ensure that fraudulent checks initiated via unauthorized access to the payroll system cannot be claimed by the perpetrator. In addition, paychecks that cannot be distributed, or are otherwise unclaimed, must not be placed under the control of the payroll department. In fact, payroll employees should not print, distribute or otherwise have access to any paychecks.

Phantom employee

A phantom employee is one that is fraudulently created via unauthorized access to the payroll system for purposes of creating a paycheck that can be claimed and cashed by a third party. The control process used to prevent such a fraud is called physical distribution, in which the check distribution process is audited by matching paychecks with identification presented by the employee to whom the check is addressed. Such a process is typically conducted periodically by employees associated with the audit function of an organization.

Reconciling output to the corresponding input data

A simple way to verify that the data that was intended to be processed was in fact processed is to use various techniques with which to compare the data input with the corresponding output. A common technique is via the use of batch controls and hash totals. Batching is the process of dividing large amounts of data into smaller subsets in order to improve manageability and control. Hash totals are assigned to each batch, consisting of manually calculated amounts that reflect the volume of data contained within the batch. Once the batch has been processed, computer generated hash totals can be used to compare to original totals to verify that all data that was intended to be processed was actually processed.

Reconciling payroll output reports to general ledger accounts and tax filing information

Balancing and reconciling is a key component of the internal controls of an organization and is intended to ensure that transactions are accurately calculated, properly classified and appropriately recognized in the books and records of the organization. As applied to a payroll organization, such activity includes the following:
- Checking payroll subsidiary accounts (based on the payroll register) with the corresponding general ledger control accounts.
- Verification of end-of-month balances between general ledger accounts and payroll system reports.
- Reconciliation of earnings and deductions registers with Form 940, *Employer's Annual Federal Unemployment (FUTA) Tax Return*, and Form 941, *Employer's Quarterly Federal Tax Return*, filings.

Reconciling payroll output reports and general ledger accounts to accounts payable activity

The typical payroll system activity of deducting amounts from employee payments creates subsequent activities for the accounts payable department: making payments of the deducted amounts to various third party payees. Examples of such items include payments to a court or other party for garnishments (such as legal settlements, child support, alimony, etc.), payments for employee-authorized withholding of charitable contributions, union dues, credit union savings, loan payments, etc., and tax payments. In order to ensure that the amount of deductions is accurate and payments are completed on a timely basis and charged to the correct accounts, reconciliations should be completed between the payroll operating reports, accounts payable reports and the accounts of the general ledger.

Security procedures for control of check fraud

Three levels of security are recommended by the American Payroll Association (APA) for the control of check fraud as follows:
1. Group 1 Security:
   a. Watermarks – visible only under certain conditions and not reproducible by copiers.
   b. Overt fibers and planchetts – visible to naked eye.
   c. Covert fibers – visible only under certain conditions.
   d. Chemical reactants - visible after contact with certain chemicals
   e. Toner bond enhancers – bonding the MICR number of checks to the paper, preventing alteration.
2. Group 2 Security:
   f. Screened printing
   g. Microprinting
   h. Simulated watermarks
   i. Warning bands
   j. Void features
   k. Prismatic printing
   l. Holograms and foils

Group 3 Security is actually a process termed Positive Pay whereby a company provides to its bank the detailed check information for each payroll including check number, payee and amount. As each check is presented for payment, it is checked against the information from the company before being processed. In this fashion, checks that do not match will not be processed.

Nondiscrimination testing for employee benefit plans

In order for an employer sponsored plan to be qualified for beneficial tax treatment (a so-called qualified plan), it must not discriminate in favor of highly compensated employees. The process of making this determination is termed nondiscrimination testing.

A plan that is found not to be discriminatory is one in which,
- The plan benefits at least 70% of all employees, and,
- At least 80% of all eligible employees participate in the plan, and
- The same benefits are available to all participants

SAS 70 audit

The Statement of Accounting Standards (SAS) #70 represents the guidance that was developed for auditors in order to perform a review of the internal controls of a service organization. In the case of a payroll organization, an audit that complies with the requirements of SAS 70 will also comply with the provisions of section 404 of the Sarbanes-Oxley Act (SOX). Section 404 of the SOX act requires that the internal controls and related business processes of a company [including the payroll operation of a company] be documented and certified as accurate by a registered public accounting firm.

Role of payroll testing for audit compliance

In a payroll operation, key components of internal control include such items as the segregation and rotation of job duties, distribution control of paychecks, control over negative deductions, control of blank check stock, time reporting and computer system edits. An audit of such activities will typically involve the following tests:
- Testing the existence of proper procedures for segregating and rotating employees.
- Testing for the custody of unclaimed paychecks and blank check stock.
- Employee physical count tests to ascertain the existence of phantom employees.
- Testing of the hours worked as reported by the time reporting system and the hours paid as reported by the payroll system.

Payroll bank reconciliation process

The typical process for reconciling the payroll account maintained at the company's bank with the corresponding account in the general ledger of the company consists of the following six steps:
1. From the general ledger account balance, add deposits recorded by the bank but not posted to the general ledger and subtract charges and fees from the bank, also not posted to the general ledger.
2. Compare each item posted in the general ledger with the bank, noting discrepancies.
3. From the bank statement, subtract the total of all uncleared checks from the ending balance of the statement.
4. Compare the adjusted balance of the general ledger to the adjusted balance of the bank statement (both should agree).
5. If they do not agree, the fun begins; research each of the items that may have improperly posted.

Accounting

Liabilities

A business liability is an obligation to pay by the business; it may be written or unwritten. The most common liabilities are accounts payable and notes payable. Trade accounts payable are unwritten promises to pay suppliers for goods or services purchased under payment terms offered by the vendor. Notes payable are formal written promises to pay creditors specific sums of money according to a fixed payment schedule, usually secured by business property. Like assets, liabilities are classified according to their life within the business operating cycle. Current liabilities include those obligations due to be paid within 12 months (or the normal operating cycle of the business, if longer). Examples of current liabilities of a business might include notes payable, accounts payable, salary payable, FICA tax payable or employee's income tax payable. Long-term liabilities are those obligations that cannot be classified as current liabilities. Mortgage Payable is an example of a liability that has both current and noncurrent components.

Assets

Assets are items of value that are owned by businesses. Cash, accounts receivable, and inventory for resale, and fixed assets such as buildings, land, machinery, and furniture and fixtures are some common business assets. Accounts receivables are unwritten customer obligations to pay at a later date for goods or services they have received Assets are grouped (cash, accounts receivable, etc.) and classified on the basis of how long it should normally take to convert them back to cash versus the entity's operating cycle (i.e. whether they are current or noncurrent). Current assets include cash and any other assets that will be converted into cash within 12 months (or the normal operating cycle of the business, if longer). Noncurrent (or long-term) assets are those that cannot be considered current assets.

Double-entry bookkeeping

Two rules of double-entry bookkeeping are: 1) every transaction should affect at least two accounts; and 2) total debits must equal total credits.

Debits and credits

First, the terms "debit" and "credit" are derivatives of Latin words for "left" and "right," respectively. This fact can facilitate an understanding of their place in modern accounting. Double entry accounting is a system that uses debits and credits to record transactions while keeping the books balanced. For each transaction recorded, total debits recorded should equal total credits recorded. This means that at least two accounts will be affected for each transaction recorded. Under the double entry system of accounting, an amount entered on the left side of the account is said to be debited; an amount entered on the right side of the account is said to be credited. The account balance is the difference between the total account debits and the total account credits.

Capital

The financial meaning of the word "capital" can vary according to the audience and the intended purpose. When used concerning business equity, capital represents the owner's investment in the business, and is the amount by which total assets exceed total liabilities. Capital is also known as owner's equity or net worth. It is composed of cash and other property contributed to the business by the owner, plus any profits generated by the business and retained for its use, less any withdrawals of equity distributed to the owner.

Trial balances

A trial balance lists all of the accounts in the entity's Chart of Accounts, showing the title and balance of each account. The balance of any account is the net effect of the total debits and total credits posted to the account. Before using a trial balance, totals for the debit and credit columns should be checked to ensure they are equal or "in balance."Asset and expense accounts normally have debit balances. Liability, owner's equity and revenue accounts normally have credit balances. The trial balance can be used to detect problems that require further investigation, as when debits and credits are out of balance, or when accounts balances do not appear in their normal debit or credit position.

Payroll journal entries

There are two basic types of employer payroll entries: paying the employees, and paying the payroll taxes. Here is an example: Employees earn $100,000 for the month, and are paid on April 30. Withholding amounts are as follows:

Federal Income Taxes	$15,000
State Income Taxes	$ 6,000
FICA Taxes	$ 7,650

After withholdings, the employees' net pay was $71,350.

1/31 Salary Expense	Debit	100,000	
Federal Income Taxes Payable	Credit	15,000	
State Income Taxes Payable	Credit	6,000	
FICA Taxes Payable	Credit	7,650	
Cash	Credit	71,350	

Assuming state unemployment taxes are $1,500 and FUTA are $500, the employer would record the following payroll tax entry:

1/31 Payroll Tax Expense	Debit	9,650
FICA Taxes Payable	Credit	7,650
State Unemp. Taxes Payable	Credit	1,500
Federal Unemp. Taxes Payable	Credit	500

Balance sheet equation

The balance sheet equation (or accounting equation) is simply stated as
        Assets = Liabilities + Equity
This equation recognizes that equity is the net effect of what the entity owns and what it owes.

Vacation and sick time accruals

Vacation and sick leave are commonly provided as employee benefits by employers. Each employee "accrues" or accumulates additional sick or vacation time at the beginning of each specified period (for instance, each month) and this time is accounted for separately. Once the accumulated time is available for employee use, the employer or the employer's payroll provider will track the amount of time used for sick leave or vacation and deduct it from the balance available. Published policies for accrual and use of sick leave and vacation ensure that all employees are treated fairly with regard to the distribution and use of sick and vacation time. Guidelines may specify the rate at which employees accumulate vacation or sick leave; often the rate is determined by length of service (the amount of time the employee has worked for the employer).

Adjusting entries for accruals and reversals

Adjusting entries may be used to accrue the effect of future transactions or defer the effect of prior transactions. Financial statements thereby better reflect the period in which those transactions occurred, regardless of when the physical receipt or expenditure of cash occurred. Reversing entries are used, in the case of accruals, to offset the physical receipt or expenditure of cash in the period it occurs. By using accrual and reversing entries, the transaction is reflected in the proper period and is not reflected twice. For instance, an invoice may be received in February for a service delivered in late January. The customer's general accounting department prepares a journal entry to accrue the cost in January (the month the service is received). In February, the accrual is reversed when the actual invoice is received and entered by the customer's accounts payable department. The entry into Accounts Payable becomes a new accrual that will effectively be reversed when the invoice is finally paid.

Trial periods and carryovers in accruing vacation and/or sick time

Many company leave policies include a provision for a trial period (or "probationary period," usually 30 to 90 days) where no time is awarded to the employee. Any leave taken (a sick day, for instance) is unpaid during this period. After this trial period, the award of leave time may begin to accrue or it may be retroactive to the date of hire. Some accrual policies include the ability to carry over or roll over some or all of the leave balance into the next year. If not, any accrued leave balance is usually lost at the end of the employer's calendar year (a "use-it-or-lose-it" provision).

Matching concept

The matching concept asserts that revenues should be reflected in the same period as the costs incurred to generate them. The matching concept is intertwined with the use of accrual based accounting.

Going concern

The going concern concept, simply stated, assumes that the business entity is financially viable and will continue in existence into the foreseeable future.

Financial statement components

The main components of a financial statement are the balance sheet; income statement; statement of changes in equity; and statement of cash flows. The balance sheet shows the financial strength and position of the company at a given point in time. The income statement reports on the entity's operations for a given period of time and shows whether operations have resulted in a profit or loss. The statement of changes in equity reconciles changes in the equity section of the balance sheet that have occurred since the previous fiscal year. Changes in equity may be the result of operating profits or losses, dividends, and similar transactions. The statement of cash flows reports on the entity's annual transactions as they affected cash.

Sections of annual reports

Most annual reports can be separated into three sections: 1) the Executive Letter; 2) the Business Review; and 3) the Financial Review. The Executive Letter is an overview of the entity's business and financial performance. The Business Review summarizes recent developments, trends, and objectives relative to the entity. The Financial Review quantifies business performance in terms of dollars. The Financial Review has two major parts: 1) Discussion and Analysis; and 2) Audited Financial Statements. The Financial Review may also include supplemental information. Management explains changes in operating results between fiscal years in the Discussion and Analysis section. This discussion is primarily presented in narrative format, and accompanying graphics may be used for highlight and illustration. The audited financial statements present the operating results and financial position of the entity, along with the auditor's opinion as to the degree by which the statements fairly present this information.

Current ratio

The current ratio is one measure of the entity's financial health and solvency, found by dividing current assets by current liabilities. The higher the result, the more likely the entity will be able to satisfy all current obligations with current resources. A low current ratio, particularly one below 1:1, is often a sign of financial distress.

Balance sheet

The balance sheet presents a financial snapshot of the entity on a given date in terms of its assets, liabilities, and equity. Assets and liabilities are grouped by current and noncurrent portions. The current portion in both cases refers to the expectation that items so classified will transition to cash within 12 months or the entity's operating cycle, if longer (for example, Accounts Receivable outstanding will be collected and Accounts Payable outstanding will be paid within the requisite period – thereby impacting cash). The equity section of the balance sheet represents the net value of the entity at historic cost. Put another way, the equity section presents the direct investment of the owners, any withdrawals by the owners (either return on investment or return of investment), and the accumulated profits and losses from operations.

Quick assets

The quick ratio is a measure of the entity's financial health and solvency, measured by its ability to quickly marshal sufficient cash resources (converting certain noncash resources at or near book value) to satisfy all current obligations. Quick assets, the total of cash and cash equivalents; accounts receivable; and marketable securities, form the numerator for this ratio. The ratio denominator is current liabilities.

Statement of cash flows

The Statement of Cash Flows presents the entity's annual transactions as they affect cash. It is separated into three sections: 1) Operating; 2) Investing; and 3) Financing. Two alternate methods are used to create this statement: 1) the Direct Method; and 2) the Indirect Method. The Direct Method examines the cash effect of major classes of receipts and payments on operations (in the Operating section). The Indirect Method, by contrast, adjusts operating profit or loss for the effect of noncash transactions such as accruals, depreciation expense, etc. The Investing (asset purchases and sales, for example) and Financing (i.e., business borrowing and owner investment) sections of the statement are the same under both alternatives.

Bank statement reconciliations

Bank statement reconciliation is an important exercise for an entity because the bank statement provides third party evidence of cash inflows and outflows for a given month. Errors and discrepancies can be detected by comparing (reconciling) the bank statement to the entity's records. Good internal controls dictate that reconciliations should be performed by someone who does not have regular responsibility for receiving or disbursing cash, checks, etc., or for managing the cash account. Unfortunately, many small employers do not have sufficient staff to fully segregate functions and the advent of microcomputer accounting software has increased the ability of a single employee to perform multiple accounting functions. In such cases, the task of bank statement reconciliation should be rotated on a random basis whenever possible or, alternatively, the owner should perform this task personally.

Basic steps in reconciling a bank statement are:
- Make sure the beginning balance per bank equals the prior month ending balance per bank
- For the month in question, add any outstanding deposits to, and deduct any outstanding withdrawals from, the ending bank balance
- Add any interest earned to, and deduct any bank fees from, the entity's book balance
- Adjust the bank and book balances, compare, and resolve.

Financing activities, investing activities, and operating activities

Financing activities concern cash inflows and outflows related to creditors and investors resulting from new note obligations and debt payments, and from new owner investment and either returns of equity or returns on equity. Investing activities concern cash inflows and outflows related to asset acquisition or disposal. Operating activities concern cash inflows and outflows related to the production and delivery of goods and services as presented on the income statement.

- 106 -

Practice Test

Practice Questions

1. Which type of worker is considered a statutory employee?
    a. Accountant
    b. Real estate agent
    c. Full-time life insurance salesperson
    d. A worker from a temporary agency

2. Under the Fair Labor Standards Act (FLSA), an employer is bound to all but which of the following requirements?
    a. A minimum hourly wage
    b. Premium pay for work performed on a holiday
    c. Deductions for uniforms or tools of the trade
    d. Overtime pay

3. What is the minimum wage for an employee that receives tips for services provided?
    a. $7.25
    b. $5.12
    c. $2.13
    d. $1.75

4. Which employment tax is not required to be withheld from employee paychecks?
    a. Federal income tax
    b. Social Security
    c. Medicare
    d. Federal unemployment tax

5. What is the maximum amount of earnings that are subject to Social Security tax in 2016?
    a. $110,100
    b. $117,000
    c. $118,500
    d. $122,100

6. When might an employer gross up an employee's income?
    a. Increasing a bonus to cover extra taxes that will be owed by the employee
    b. Increasing wages to cover federal withholding taxes
    c. To pay for employee benefits such as life insurance or retirement plan contributions
    d. It is illegal for an employer to gross up employee wages

7. Which Internal Revenue Service (IRS) form is used to report an employer's Federal Unemployment tax (FUTA)?
    a. Form SS-8
    b. Form 843
    c. Form 1042
    d. Form 940

8. When must an organization collect an IRS Form W-9 from an individual?
   a. When hiring an independent contractor
   b. To enable donors to claim a tax deduction
   c. Both A and B
   d. None of the above

9. The minimum age at which an employee may operate a motor vehicle on public roads is...
   a. 16½ years of age with parental permission
   b. 17 years of age and pass driver education course
   c. 17 years of age and meeting requirements for time spent driving and vehicle weight
   d. 18 years of age

10. Under the FLSA, which test is not required for exemption as a creative professional employee?
   a. Minimum weekly salary or fee of $455 per week
   b. The work must require originality, invention or talent
   c. The work must be in a recognized field of artistic endeavor
   d. The copyright to the work must be retained by the business

11. In a shared services environment, which type of service provider performs services after coming to an agreement with the customer and bases the price on the services used?
   a. Service-oriented provider
   b. Business-based provider
   c. Contributor-valued provider
   d. Partner-integrated provider

12. What qualifies an employee for benefits under the Family and Medical Leave Act of 1993?
   a. At least 12 months working with the employer, with 1,250 hours worked within the last 12 months
   b. 1,250 hours worked within the last 12 months
   c. At least 24 months working with the employer, with 1,250 hours worked within the last 12 months
   d. 1,000 hours worked within the last 12 months

13. Which condition must be met in order for income to be constructively received by a taxpayer?
   a. Income must be paid to the taxpayer
   b. Income must be available to the taxpayer without substantial limitations
   c. Taxpayer must be notified that payment will be made
   d. Income must be taxable earnings

14. Which of the following regulates how often employees must be paid by an employer?
   a. The Fair Labor Standards Act
   b. The individual state
   c. US Department of Labor
   d. National Labor Relations Act

15. Escheat laws cover which type of check issued by a company?
    a. Payroll services
    b. Accounts payable
    c. Per diem reimbursement
    d. None of the above

16. What procedure is followed when an account has been inactive for a period of time and the company has been unable to contact the owner of the funds?
    a. Inform the state that the company is holding unclaimed property
    b. Transfer the unclaimed property to the Department of Revenue
    c. Send the unclaimed property to the state government
    d. Send the unclaimed property to a commercial escheatment provider

17. Which of the following expenses can be included in a Section 125 plan?
    a. Insurance premiums
    b. Out-of-pocket medical expenses
    c. Child care expenses
    d. All of the above

18. What is a common error employers make when reporting Social Security?
    a. The report misstates the amount of Social Security taxes collected by the employer
    b. The report contains the wrong Employer Identification Number
    c. The report inaccurately states the amount of wages paid to employees
    d. None of the above

19. Which of the following is exempt from filing a Form I-9?
    a. An employee hired by a company before 1987
    b. An employee who provides in-home health care
    c. An employer with no control of how or when the work is performed
    d. Services provided under a contract dated after 1987

20. What percentage of an employee's earnings is paid by the employer for FUTA?
    a. 6.0% of the first $7,000 earned by an employee
    b. 6.2% of the first $17,000 earned by an employee
    c. 5.4% of the first $7,000 earned by an employee
    d. 6.0% of earnings over $1,000 during a quarter

21. What are the two federal employment tax deposit schedules?
    a. Monthly and semi-annual
    b. Semi-weekly and semi-annual
    c. Monthly and semi-weekly
    d. Weekly and monthly

22. What is the period used to determine whether an employer pays employment taxes on a semi-weekly or monthly basis?
    a. The lookback period
    b. The payback period
    c. The loopback period
    d. The payloop period

23. Who should be allowed to have access to an employee's Form I-9 records?
    a. Human resources
    b. An employee's supervisor
    c. Executive management
    d. All of the above

24. For how long must an employer covered by the FLSA keep payroll records for non-exempt employees?
    a. Three years
    b. Four years
    c. Seven years
    d. For the life of the business

25. What is the maximum penalty that can be assessed against an employer that has not retained completed copies of Form I-9 for each of its non-exempt employees?
    a. $100
    b. $110
    c. $1,000
    d. $1,100

26. What is the penalty for failure to file Form W-2 if the correct Form W-2 is filed within 30 days?
    a. $15 for each W-2
    b. $30 for each W-2
    c. $50 for each W-2
    d. $100 for each W-2

27. Which of the following must be defined before overtime calculations can be made?
    a. The rate of pay
    b. The workweek
    c. The company's overtime policy
    d. The overtime contract with the employee

28. Which statement about imputed income is NOT true?
    a. Imputed income is subject to federal income tax withholding rules
    b. Imputed income is subject to withholding for FICA tax purposes
    c. Using an employer-provided asset for personal use can be classified as imputed income
    d. The employee's W-2 must include imputed income

29. Which of the following federal taxes is not withheld from an employee's wages after the employee's death?
    a. Social Security
    b. Medicare
    c. FUTA
    d. Federal Income Tax Withholding

30. Under the Consumer Credit Protection Act of 1977, what percentage of an employee's disposable earnings can be deducted if the employee supports two families and is 12 or more weeks in arrears on child support?
    a. 50%
    b. 55%
    c. 60%
    d. 65%

31. What characteristic makes a cafeteria plan different from other types of benefit plans?
    a. Cafeteria plans offer accident benefits
    b. The employee has a choice of only nontaxable benefits
    c. The employee has a choice between taxable and nontaxable benefits
    d. Cafeteria plans offer only health benefits

32. Which type of flexible benefit plan provides compulsory coverage for key benefits?
    a. Cafeteria plan
    b. Core plus plan
    c. Traditional plan
    d. Modular plan

33. Which of the following employers would be exempt from filing an IRS Form 940?
    a. A household or agricultural employer
    b. One that pays less than $1,500 a year in wages
    c. One that employs a person for less than 20 days
    d. All of the above

34. A "monthly schedule depositor" refers to...
    a. how often a business pays its employees
    b. how often a business is required to make tax deposits
    c. the set of deposit rules that apply to an employer
    d. the date on which an employer pays its employees

35. The overtime premium for a commission-only employee who worked 50 hours in a week and earned $1,000 in commissions would be...
    a. $300
    b. $200
    c. $100
    d. None

36. A reason for grossing up net paycheck amounts might be to...
    a. provide the employee with a temporary raise
    b. cover an employee's moving expenses
    c. reimburse an employee for employee-paid insurance premiums
    d. pay the employee's withholding and social security taxes on a taxable benefit

37. When considering the purchase of a payroll system for a construction company, which system ability would be considered necessary?
    a. Compliance with Davis-Bacon prevailing wage requirements
    b. Compliance with labor union wage negotiations
    c. Compliance with overtime regulations
    d. Completion of federal tax forms

38. The purpose of a checksum in a software backup program is to...
    a. ensure that all files have been backed up
    b. determine the date of the last backup
    c. identify identical files in a backup
    d. ensure the data integrity of the backup data

39. Which type of feasibility study addresses budgetary constraints?
    a. An operational feasibility study
    b. A technical feasibility study
    c. An economic feasibility study
    d. A schedule feasibility study

40. What is the major factor that determines the amount of data loss a business may be willing to tolerate?
    a. Data importance
    b. Cost
    c. Recovery time
    d. Backup storage requirements

41. Adjusting entries are used to...
    a. record items that were not recorded in the correct time period
    b. accrue the effect of future transactions
    c. defer the effect of prior transactions
    d. Both B and C

42. Which is not a component of a financial statement?
    a. Balance sheet
    b. Income Statement
    c. Statement of changes in assets
    d. Statement of cash flow

43. Performing a bank reconciliation is important to...
    a. ensure the accuracy of the cash account
    b. detect errors and discrepancies
    c. catch errors in the bank's records
    d. determine uncleared cash items

44. Implementing internal control systems for payroll is important to...
    a. ensure timely payment to employees
    b. accurately record payroll taxes
    c. ensure payroll taxes are paid on time
    d. reduce uncorrected errors and theft

45. Which of the following is not normally included in the job description for payroll personnel?
    a. Company information
    b. Major functional areas and responsibilities
    c. Minimum qualifications
    d. Physical requirements

46. What is the most important quality of a payroll manager when dealing with changes in an organization?
    a. Flexibility in scheduling time
    b. Ability to change with the organization
    c. Ability to deal with employee attitudes regarding the changes
    d. Leadership ability

47. What is the basic premise of the matching concept used in accounting?
    a. Expenses are accrued until paid
    b. Revenues are reflected at the same time as associated costs
    c. Debits must equal credits
    d. Cash entries have a matching expense entry

48. How is an organization's quick ratio measured?
    a. Current assets divided by total liabilities
    b. Current liabilities divided by current assets
    c. Current assets divided by current liabilities
    d. Current liabilities divided by total assets

49. Which set of organizational activities would be most concerned with cash flow from debt?
    a. Financing activities
    b. Investing activities
    c. Operating activities
    d. Marketing activities

50. Which skill is essential for good performance management?
    a. Leadership
    b. Delegation
    c. Teamwork
    d. Communication

Answers and Explanations

1. C: Full-time life insurance salesperson. A statutory employee is a self-employed person, considered an employee for tax purposes. Other types of statutory employees include:
- Delivery drivers that are agents of a company, or paid on commission
- Individuals that work at home with materials supplied by a company
- Full-time traveling salespersons that sells products for resale to other businesses

An accountant may be considered an independent contractor if services are provided to several clients. A real estate agent would be considered a statutory non-employee if compensation is based on sales and not on hours worked. A worker that is hired from a temporary agency is considered a leased employee.

2. B: Premium pay for work performed on a holiday. The Fair Labor Standards Act (FLSA) pertains to covered, non-exempt workers and entitles these workers to:
- A minimum wage, currently at $7.25 per hour
- Overtime pay after 40 hours work, paid at 1.5 times the worker's regular pay
- A regular payday

Deductions for uniforms and tools are allowed as long as wages are not reduced below minimum wage. The FLSA does not require employers to pay employees the following:
- Paid vacations, holidays, meal times and rest periods
- Severance pay, sick pay, pay raises and fringe benefits
- Premium pay for work performed on the weekend or holidays
- A notice or reason for discharge

3. C: $2.13. The federal minimum wage for covered, non-exempt employees is $7.25 per hour. However, an employer may pay a tipped employee a minimum wage of $2.13 per hour if:
- The hourly rate plus tips received by the employee equal the federal minimum wage
- The tips are retained by the employee
- The employee receives more than $30 a month in tips

If the $2.13 per hour plus tips does not equal the federal minimum wage, the employer must pay the employee the difference.

4. D: Federal unemployment tax. Federal unemployment taxes are not deducted from employee paychecks. They, along with state unemployment taxes, are paid by the employer only. Federal income taxes are paid by the employee, but withheld from the employee's paycheck by the employer. Social Security and Medicare are paid by both the employer and the employee.

5. C: $118,500. Employees are only required to pay Social Security taxes on the first $118,500 of income earned in 2016. This is referred to as the contribution and benefit base, or taxable maximum. Wages above this amount are not subject to Social Security Tax. There is no limitation on taxable earnings for Medicare's Hospital Insurance program. Any employee who pays more than the maximum tax required is eligible for a refund of the excess contribution.

6. A: Increasing a bonus to cover extra taxes that will be owed by the employee. There are two situations where an employer may gross up an employee's paycheck, both of which are to cover additional taxes incurred by an employee— either from a bonus payment or from a taxable fringe benefit. By grossing up an employee's compensation, the employee receives a certain amount without having to pay part of that bonus or benefit as taxes. Though it may appear that the employer is paying the employee's tax liability; the taxes are collected from, and paid by, the employee.

7. D: Form 940. Form 940 is used to report an employer's annual Federal Unemployment tax (FUTA) obligation. FUTA, in combination with state unemployment tax, is used to provide unemployment compensation to workers that have lost their jobs. FUTA tax is paid only by employers, and is not deducted from an employee's paycheck. An employer must pay FUTA tax on the first $7,000 of each employee's annual earnings. For household employees, FUTA tax is only paid if the employee receives wages of $1,000 or more in a calendar quarter.

8. C: Both A and B. Internal Revenue Service (IRS) Form W-9 is used by businesses to obtain the taxpayer identification number of an independent contractor. The form is also used by non-profit organizations to collect the taxpayer identification number of a donor, so that the donor can deduct the donation on its tax return. Form W-9 is not submitted to the IRS, but instead kept on file by the organization and used when preparing Form 1099s. Information collected on form W-9 includes:
- The independent contractor's, or donor's, name or business name
- Address
- Type of business
- Social Security number (for individuals) or federal employer identification number (EIN for businesses)
- Signature of the independent contractor or donor

9. C: 17 years of age and meeting requirements for time spent driving and vehicle weight. Under the FLSA child labor provisions, a 17-year-old may drive a motor vehicle on public roads after meeting requirements for the amount of time spent driving the vehicle and the weight of the vehicle. Employees under age 17 years may not drive on public roads. The 17-year-old may not leave the vehicle because employees under age 18 cannot be an outside helper on a motor vehicle. Outside helpers are employees that must leave the vehicle, or who ride outside the vehicle to deliver or assist in transporting goods.

10. D: The copyright to the work must be retained by the business. Under the FLSA, employers are not required to provide overtime pay for certain "exempt" occupations, such as those falling under the categories "learned professional" or "creative professional." As a general rule, employees who are paid less than $455 per week are non-exempt and entitled to overtime pay. An employee must also pass one of the following duties tests:
- Exempt executive job duties— a full-time manager that supervises two or more employees
- Exempt professional job duties— learned professions that require advanced degrees and creative professionals that use imagination or talent to create a work
- Exempt administrative job duties— administrative employees that assist executive management

11. B: Business-based provider. In a shared services environment, there are four types of providers:
- A business-based provider performs services after coming to an agreement with the customer and bases the price on the services used
- A service-oriented provider knows in advance what the customer expects, provides performance measurements and meets customer expectations
- A contributor-valued provider has a defined level of accountability and responsibility with payment commensurate with services delivered
- A partner-integrated provider anticipates new service needs and contributes to the customer's profitability.

12. A: At least 12 months working with the employer, with 1,250 hours worked within the last 12 months. The Family and Medical Leave Act (FMLA) mandates unpaid leave to employees for family or medical reasons, in businesses with 50 or more employees. The FMLA provides unpaid, job-protected leave for a maximum of 12 weeks. The employer must also provide the following while the employee is on leave:
- Identical health insurance benefits
- The same or similar position when the employee returns to work
- Protection of employee benefits, and reinstatement of benefits when the employee returns to work
- Protection of the employee's rights under the Act
- Protection from retaliation by the employer

13. B: Income must be available to the taxpayer without substantial limitations. Constructive receipt determines when a taxpayer who receives income on a cash-basis has received that income. Income considered to be received by the taxpayer is that which is made available with no substantial limitations placed on the taxpayer having access to that income. The taxpayer need not have actual physical control of the income. Even though the income may not be under the taxpayer's control, the following scenarios make income considered to have been constructively received by the taxpayer:
- The funds have been credited to an account on behalf of the taxpayer
- The funds have been set apart for the taxpayer
- The taxpayer may make a draw against the funds at any time

14. B: The individual state. The frequency of payments made to an employee by an employer is regulated by the state in which the work is performed. The individual states also determine the length of time in which an employer must pay an employee after such wages have been earned.

15. A: Payroll services. Escheat laws pertain to unclaimed or abandoned property. This property may be held in, among other places, accounts at financial institutions and companies. To be classified as unclaimed, there must have been no activity in the account, or no contact with the owner, for one year or more. Common forms of unclaimed property include bank accounts, stocks, uncashed payroll checks, trust distributions, unredeemed money orders or gift certificates, insurance payments, annuities, Certificates of Deposit, utility security deposits, and contents of safe deposit boxes.
Payroll obligations that may be covered by state escheat laws include wages, commissions, bonuses, returnable garnishments, deferred compensation and payroll services.

16. C: Send the unclaimed property to the state government. Depending on state law, funds held by a company on behalf of an employee may be considered unclaimed if the account has been inactive for between three and five years. The amount of time depends on state law. The company must also file the appropriate forms, as specified by state law, by a designated date. In addition, the business must reconcile the reported unclaimed property amounts to the source documents relating to the unclaimed amounts.

17. D: All of the above. Section 125 plans are also called cafeteria plans. These benefit plans allow an employee a budget of $5,000 to spend on the following plan components:
- Insurance premiums for health, dental, vision, accident, life, cancer and hospital
- Out-of-pocket medical expenses
- Child care expenses

The cafeteria plan can be funded by either the employer or the employee, but the employee chooses how much to spend in each component of the plan. Cafeteria plans can reduce an employee's tax liability. The money contributed into the plan by the employee is exempt from income tax. The IRS requires 70% of an employer's eligible employees participate in the out-of-pocket medical expenses component of the plan.

18. B: The report contains the wrong Employer Identification Number. There are a number of errors commonly made by employers when reporting Social Security taxes. These errors include:
- Reports contain an erroneous Employer Identification Numbers (EIN). The Social Security Administration (SSA) and IRS maintain employer records by EIN. If the wrong EIN is used, amounts reported may be credited to the wrong employer. A missing or incorrect EIN may result in the IRS assessing penalties.
- Employee names and Social Security numbers are incorrect. To properly credit reported earnings, the SSA must match the employee name and Social Security number on the wage report to the name and number in its files.

19. C: The employer does not have control of how or when the work is performed. U.S. employers must have every employee complete and sign an IRS Form I-9. This form is retained by the company in its files. Companies are not required to obtain a Form I-9 from an employee under the following circumstances:
- The employee was hired before Nov. 7, 1986, and has been continuously employed by the same employer
- The employee provides domestic services in a private household on a sporadic, irregular, or intermittent basis
- The services are provided as an independent contractor. An independent contractor conducts an independent business and contracts to do work using its own methods. It is subject to control only with respect to results. The employer does not set work hours, provide any tools, or have authority to hire and fire
- The services are provided under a contract, subcontract, or exchange entered into after Nov. 6, 1986. The contractor is the employer for I-9 purposes. This applies to contractors such as temporary employment agencies

20. A: 6.0% of the first $7,000 earned by an employee. IRS Form 940 is used to report taxes paid by the employer to provide for unemployment compensation to workers who have lost their jobs. Employers must pay federal unemployment tax (FUTA) on behalf of its employees. FUTA is not deducted from an employee's earnings. The employer pays 6.0% on

the first $7,000 earned by an employee in a year, and up to 5.4% of state unemployment payments may be applied to an employer's FUTA liability. An employer must pay FUTA on household employees that earned more than $1,000 during any quarter during the year.

21. C: Monthly and semi-weekly. The two deposit schedules are monthly and semi-weekly. Employers deposit their Social Security, Medicare, and withheld income taxes according to these schedules, telling the employer when a deposit is due after a tax liability arises (for example, when employees have a payday). Before the beginning of each calendar year, employers must determine which of the two deposit schedules they are required to use. The deposit schedule that must be used is based on the total tax liability that was reported on IRS Form 941 during a four-quarter lookback period. The deposit schedule is not determined by how often employees are paid.

22. A: The lookback period. The lookback period determines the amount of employment taxes paid by an employer. The amount of taxes paid determines whether the employer pay federal employment taxes on a semi-weekly or monthly basis. For IRS purposes, the lookback period is the aggregate amount of federal employment taxes reported by an employer in the 12-month period ending June 30. Employers that report $50,000 or less in taxes for the lookback period are required to deposit employment taxes on a monthly basis. Employers that report more than $50,000 are required to deposit employment taxes on a semi-weekly basis.

23. A: Human resources. Employers are required to have employees complete and sign the Employment Eligibility Verification Form I-9. The U.S. Citizenship and Immigration Services (USCIS) uses this form to verify that employees are legally authorized to work in the US. All Form I-9s collected by a company should be placed in a separate file, and not in the employee's personnel files. This helps ensure that employee personnel records remain confidential in the event that USCIS elects to inspect these forms. In addition, employees' Form I-9 records should only be made available to a company's human resources and auditing departments, and to investigative agencies.

24. A: Three years. Under FLSA regulations, employers must retain payroll records for each non-exempt employee for a period of three years. This information includes:
- Name, last known address and social security number
- Amount of wages paid to the employee for each payroll period, deductions, and the date of payment

The following records satisfy the retention requirement:
- Individual employee earnings card or record showing earnings and deductions for each pay period
- Master payroll register showing earnings and deductions for each pay period
- Copies of annual or other periodic statements furnished to each employee detailing deductions and contributions to pension or deferred compensation plans during the past year or period

25. D: $1,100. Employers who do not properly complete, retain or present Forms I-9 for inspection as required by law may be subject to civil penalties. For violations occurring on or after Sept. 29, 1999, the penalty can range from $110 - $1,100 per each employee whose Form I-9 is not properly completed, retained or presented. For violations occurring before Sept. 29, 1999, civil penalties range from $100 to $1,000. In determining the amount of the civil penalty, the following factors are considered:

- The size of the business of the employer being charged
- The good faith of the employer and the severity of the violation
- Whether or not the individual was an unauthorized alien
- The history of previous violations by the employer

26. A: $15 for each W-2. Businesses can incur penalties if they fail to file a correct IRS Form W-2 by the due date. Penalties apply when a W-2 is not filed on time, does not contain required information or includes incorrect information. The amount of the penalty is based on when the correct W-2 is filed. The penalty is:
- $15 per W-2 if correctly filed within 30 days
- $30 per W-2 if correctly filed more than 30 days after the due date
- $50 per W-2 if required W-2s are not filed

Penalties will not be charged if any of the following exceptions apply:
- The failure was due to reasonable cause and not to willful neglect
- An inconsequential error or omission is not a failure to include correct information

27. B: The workweek. The workweek is defined as seven consecutive 24-hour periods. The only requirement of a workweek is that the day of the week that the workweek starts stays the same and that the workweek is a fixed and regularly-occurring period of 168 hours. Under the FLSA, non-exempt employees are entitled to receive overtime pay for any hours worked over 40 hours in any one workweek. It is at the employer's discretion when to start the workweek and the workweek can vary among different employees of the same employer. Once the workweek that applies to overtime calculations is defined, then the hours worked by the employee can be determined.

28. A: Imputed income is subject to federal income tax withholding rules. Imputed income is the addition of the value of cash or non-cash compensation to an employee's taxable wages, Employer-paid tuition reimbursement and other fringe benefits fall under the category of imputed income, as would the personal use of a company-provided vehicle. Other common examples include:
- Group term taxable life insurance coverage over $50,000
- Dependent-care assistance exceeding the tax-free amount
- Non-deductible relocation expenses reimbursement

Imputed income is included in the employee's Form W-2, but not subject to federal income tax withholding rules. It is, however, subject to FICA withholding. Employees have the option of having federal income tax withheld on the imputed income or pay the tax due when filing their income tax returns.

29. D: Federal Income Tax Withholding. Following the death of an employee, it is the employer's responsibility to determine wages owed to the employee's estate and to deduct the appropriate taxes. Amounts due to the employee may include current wages, accrued vacation and bonuses. Deductions are made for Social Security, Medicare and FUTA because the employee had earned income that should be credited toward those benefits. Federal Income tax is not withheld because the income is taxable against the employee's estate or beneficiary.

30. B: 55%. Under the Consumer Credit Protection Act (CCPA), the amount that can be withheld from an employee's wages is limited depending on certain criteria:

- If the employee supports a second family and is less than 12 weeks in arrears on child support, 50% of disposable wages can be used to pay the current child support
- If the employee supports a second family and is 12 weeks or more in arrears on child support, 55% of disposable wages can be used to pay the current child support
- If the employee does not support a second family and is less than 12 weeks in arrears on child support, 60% of disposable wages can be used to pay the current child support
- If the employee does not support a second family and is 12 or more weeks in arrears on child support, 65% of disposable wages can be used to pay the current child support

Disposable earnings are an employee's gross earnings less deductions for withholding for income taxes, Social Security, Medicare and unemployment taxes.

31. C: The employee has a choice between taxable and nontaxable benefits. Cafeteria plans fall under section 125 of the Internal Revenue Code. Cafeteria plans give employers the option to offer employees certain benefits on a pre-tax basis. In a cafeteria plan, employees can choose from at least one taxable benefit and one qualified benefit. Qualified benefits do not defer compensation and are excluded from the employee's gross income. Some examples of qualified benefits are:
- Accident and health benefits
- Health savings accounts
- Group term life insurance
- Dependent care assistance
- Adoption assistance

32. B: Core plus plan. There are four types of flexible benefit plans that may be made available to employees:
- Cafeteria plans offer employees the greatest number of choices and options. Employees are able to design their own plan within certain spending limits, based on their needs. This type of plan is usually paid by the employer
- Core plus plans provide required benefits such as life, disability and catastrophic health coverage. The plans offer employees other benefits that may be paid for by the employee
- Traditional plans offer employees the option of purchasing additional coverage or having an account from which health and dental expenses can be paid
- Modular plans are the simplest type of flexible benefit plan, giving the employee a choice of different plans

33. D: All of the above. IRS Form 940 is used by employers to report the employer's annual Federal Unemployment Tax (FUTA) liability to the IRS. Nearly all businesses are responsible for filing Form 940. Employers are exempt if it:
- Is a household or agricultural employer
- Pays less than $1,500 a year in wages
- Employs an individual for less than 20 days each year

34. C: The set of deposit rules that apply to an employer. There are two deposit schedules— monthly or semiweekly— from which employers determine when to deposit their Social Security, Medicare, and withheld income taxes. New employers who have never filed IRS Forms 941 or 944 before automatically become monthly schedule depositors for their first

calendar year of business. These employers will deposit taxes from all their paydays in a given month by the 15th of the next month. An exception occurs if an employer has accumulated $100,000 in payroll taxes during a deposit period, in which case, the deposit must be made in the next business day after that $100,000 mark has been reached. Moving forward, after the first calendar year with four quarters of operational history having passed, the deposit schedule can then be based on the total tax liability that was reported on Form 941 during a four-quarter lookback period.

35. C: $100. The employee earned $1,000 working 50 hours, making the pay per hour $20 (1,000 divided by 50). The overtime premium is calculated by taking the 10 hours overtime worked by the employee multiplied by $10 ($20 per hour divided by ½).

36. D: Pay the employee's withholding and Social Security taxes on a taxable benefit. "Grossing up" is the calculating of the gross equivalent of a net amount. When an employer grosses up an employee's paycheck, the taxes paid by the employer are included in the employee's taxable income. Typical circumstances in which grossing up is used include:
- Employee bonuses— the employer wants the employee to receive the full bonus, and will gross up the bonus to cover the employee's withholding taxes on the amount of the bonus
- Relocation expenses— the employer pays the employee's taxes on taxable relocation expenses
- The value of a taxable benefit for a terminated employee is calculated but Social Security tax or Medicare tax was not withheld

37. A: Compliance with Davis-Bacon prevailing wage requirements. The Davis-Bacon and Related Acts requires contractors working on US federal government projects to pay employees at least the prevailing wage and benefits received by workers employed in similar projects in the geographic area. Thus, a construction company can have fairly complex payroll needs, among them the ability to comply with Davis-Bacon by researching various jobs and their wages. Other features a payroll system for a construction company might need are:
- The ability to allocate indirect cost based on labor
- The ability to handle requirements of multiple unions and multiple collective bargaining contracts
- The ability to process mid-payroll checks for employees whose employment is voluntarily or involuntarily terminated during the middle of a payroll period in construction jobs

38. D: Ensure the data integrity of the backup data. Many backup programs utilize checksums or hashes. This allows data integrity to be verified without reference to the original file. If the file, as stored on the backup medium, has the same checksum as the saved value, then it's probable that data integrity has been maintained in the copy. Some backup programs can use checksums to reduce the need for redundant copies of files, which helps to improve backup speed. This is particularly useful when backing up multiple workstations over a network, since each workstation may contain its own copy of the same file. If the backup software detects several copies of a file having the same size, date stamp, and checksum, it can backup one copy of the data and include metadata listing all network locations where copies of this file were found.

39. B: A technical feasibility study. The feasibility study phase of an information system project should consider the present system; users, policies, functions, objectives, failures or problems with the existing system. Then, objectives and other requirements for the new system can be formulated. There are four types of feasibility studies:
- Technical feasibility— addressing technological, budgetary, and related constraints
- Operational feasibility— addressing personnel, regulatory, and other logistics
- Economic feasibility— addressing costs of the project versus the benefits derived
- Schedule feasibility— addressing concerns related to project effort scheduling and completion

40. B: Cost. There is an inverse relationship between the amount of data a business can afford to lose and the requirements of a backup and disaster recovery plan. The degree of inverse correlation may vary according to industry, company, and situation. A large bank can't afford to lose even one transaction. In other cases, the business may be able to follow the paper trail to recapture activity for a limited period of time. Often, cost is a primary factor in determining the degree of risk of potential data loss the business is willing to assume.

41. D: Both B and C. Adjusting entries may be used to accrue the effect of future transactions or defer the effect of prior transactions. This results in financial statements better reflecting the periods in which those transactions occurred, regardless of when the physical receipt or expenditure of cash occurred. In the case of accruals, reversing entries are used to offset the physical receipt or expenditure of cash in the period it occurs. By using accrual and reversing entries, the transaction is reflected in the proper period, and is not duplicated.

42. C: Statement of changes in assets. The main components of a financial statement are:
- The balance sheet— shows the financial strength and position of the company at a given point in time through the listing of assets and liabilities
- The income statement— reports on the entity's operations for a given period of time and shows whether operations have resulted in a profit or loss
- The statement of changes in equity— reconciles changes in the equity section of the balance sheet that have occurred since the previous fiscal year. Changes in equity may be the result of operating profits or losses, dividends, and similar transactions
- The statement of cash flows—reports on the entity's annual transactions as they affected cash

43. B: Detect errors and discrepancies. Bank statement reconciliation enables a business to detect errors and discrepancies by comparing the bank statement to the business' internal records. The bank statement provides solid third party evidence of cash inflows and outflows for a given period. Good internal controls within a business dictate that reconciliations be performed by a person who does not have regular responsibility for receiving or disbursing funds or managing the cash account. Basic steps in reconciling a bank statement are:
- Making sure the beginning balance equals the prior month's ending balance per bank
- For the month in question, add any outstanding deposits to, and deduct any outstanding withdrawals from, the ending bank balance
- Add any interest earned to, and deduct any bank fees from, the entity's book balance
- Adjust the bank and book balances, compare, and resolve

44. D: Reduce uncorrected errors and theft. Internal controls are established in payroll to reduce the chance of uncorrected errors and theft. Good internal controls normally include a system of checks and balances requiring adequate documentation to support entries to the payroll system, such as a timecard, timesheet, or other document to support time worked. They also focus on transaction verification by other personnel, helping to determine, for example, if a timecard was entered correctly. Good internal controls should also spell out a separation of function, so that, for example, the person entering timecard information is not the same person who disburses checks.

45. D: Physical requirements. A job description for payroll personnel might be written using the following generic template:
- Brief paragraph about company or unit: its mission, size, and summary of position role within unit. Also indicates level of supervision received
- Major functional areas, including specific responsibilities in each of those areas (brief outline or narrative)
- Minimum qualifications such as education, experience, special training and job related accomplishments

46. D: Leadership ability. Good leadership, above all, helps an organization effectively manage a changing environment. Payroll personnel are often queried in a changing environment due to their proximity to the compensation. Change is a common occurrence in business today, and solid change management skills are a large component of leadership, today more than ever. To be an effective leader in the change management process, it helps if you:
- Set an example— if you want others in your business to change, you must set an example for them to follow
- Eliminate perks— by eliminating or reducing your own perks, you show your desire to level the playing field
- Be genuine— as a leader of change, it is important to be as real and honest as possible in your interactions with others

Leadership development hinges on your ability to get people to believe in you. Knowing about the psychological stages people experience in a changing environment will also help affect a successful transition.

47. B: Revenues are reflected at the same time as associated costs. The matching concept asserts that revenues should be reflected in the same period as the costs incurred to generate them. The matching concept is intertwined with the use of accrual based accounting.

48. C: Current assets divided by current liabilities. The quick ratio is a measure of the entity's financial health and solvency, measured by its ability to quickly marshal sufficient cash resources (converting certain non-cash resources at or near book value) to satisfy all current obligations. Quick assets, the total of cash and cash equivalents; accounts receivable; and marketable securities, form the numerator for this ratio. The ratio denominator is current liabilities.

49. A: Financing activities. Financing activities concern cash inflows and outflows related to creditors and investors resulting from new note obligations and debt payments, and from

new owner investment and either returns of equity or returns on equity. Investing activities concern cash inflows and outflows related to asset acquisition or disposal. Operating activities concern cash inflows and outflows related to the production and delivery of goods and services as presented on the income statement.

50. D: Communication. Excellent communication skills are essential for good performance management. They are important competencies used in the entire performance management process, from planning and communicating work expectations to recognizing employees for their successful achievements. To communicate effectively with employees, performance managers must:

- Establish strong working relationships with employees
- Promote easy access to information and feedback
- Promote employee involvement in planning and development activities
- Recognize and praise top performers

Secret Key #1 - Time is Your Greatest Enemy

Pace Yourself

Wear a watch. At the beginning of the test, check the time (or start a chronometer on your watch to count the minutes), and check the time after every few questions to make sure you are "on schedule."

If you are forced to speed up, do it efficiently. Usually one or more answer choices can be eliminated without too much difficulty. Above all, don't panic. Don't speed up and just begin guessing at random choices. By pacing yourself, and continually monitoring your progress against your watch, you will always know exactly how far ahead or behind you are with your available time. If you find that you are one minute behind on the test, don't skip one question without spending any time on it, just to catch back up. Take 15 fewer seconds on the next four questions, and after four questions you'll have caught back up. Once you catch back up, you can continue working each problem at your normal pace.

Furthermore, don't dwell on the problems that you were rushed on. If a problem was taking up too much time and you made a hurried guess, it must be difficult. The difficult questions are the ones you are most likely to miss anyway, so it isn't a big loss. It is better to end with more time than you need than to run out of time.

Lastly, sometimes it is beneficial to slow down if you are constantly getting ahead of time. You are always more likely to catch a careless mistake by working more slowly than quickly, and among very high-scoring test takers (those who are likely to have lots of time left over), careless errors affect the score more than mastery of material.

Secret Key #2 - Guessing is not Guesswork

You probably know that guessing is a good idea. Unlike other standardized tests, there is no penalty for getting a wrong answer. Even if you have no idea about a question, you still have a 20-25% chance of getting it right.

Most test takers do not understand the impact that proper guessing can have on their score. Unless you score extremely high, guessing will significantly contribute to your final score.

Monkeys Take the Test

What most test takers don't realize is that to insure that 20-25% chance, you have to guess randomly. If you put 20 monkeys in a room to take this test, assuming they answered once per question and behaved themselves, on average they would get 20-25% of the questions correct. Put 20 test takers in the room, and the average will be much lower among guessed questions. Why?

1. The test writers intentionally write deceptive answer choices that "look" right. A test taker has no idea about a question, so he picks the "best looking" answer, which is often wrong. The monkey has no idea what looks good and what doesn't, so it will consistently be right about 20-25% of the time.
2. Test takers will eliminate answer choices from the guessing pool based on a hunch or intuition. Simple but correct answers often get excluded, leaving a 0% chance of being correct. The monkey has no clue, and often gets lucky with the best choice.

This is why the process of elimination endorsed by most test courses is flawed and detrimental to your performance. Test takers don't guess; they make an ignorant stab in the dark that is usually worse than random.

$5 Challenge

Let me introduce one of the most valuable ideas of this course—the $5 challenge:

You only mark your "best guess" if you are willing to bet $5 on it.
You only eliminate choices from guessing if you are willing to bet $5 on it.

Why $5? Five dollars is an amount of money that is small yet not insignificant, and can really add up fast (20 questions could cost you $100). Likewise, each answer choice on one question of the test will have a small impact on your overall score, but it can really add up to a lot of points in the end.

The process of elimination IS valuable. The following shows your chance of guessing it right:

If you eliminate wrong answer choices until only this many remain:	Chance of getting it correct:
1	100%
2	50%
3	33%

However, if you accidentally eliminate the right answer or go on a hunch for an incorrect answer, your chances drop dramatically—to 0%. By guessing among all the answer choices, you are GUARANTEED to have a shot at the right answer.

That's why the $5 test is so valuable. If you give up the advantage and safety of a pure guess, it had better be worth the risk.

What we still haven't covered is how to be sure that whatever guess you make is truly random. Here's the easiest way:

Always pick the first answer choice among those remaining.

Such a technique means that you have decided, **before you see a single test question**, exactly how you are going to guess, and since the order of choices tells you nothing about which one is correct, this guessing technique is perfectly random.

This section is not meant to scare you away from making educated guesses or eliminating choices; you just need to define when a choice is worth eliminating. The $5 test, along with a pre-defined random guessing strategy, is the best way to make sure you reap all of the benefits of guessing.

Secret Key #3 - Practice Smarter, Not Harder

Many test takers delay the test preparation process because they dread the awful amounts of practice time they think necessary to succeed on the test. We have refined an effective method that will take you only a fraction of the time.

There are a number of "obstacles" in the path to success. Among these are answering questions, finishing in time, and mastering test-taking strategies. All must be executed on the day of the test at peak performance, or your score will suffer. The test is a mental marathon that has a large impact on your future.

Just like a marathon runner, it is important to work your way up to the full challenge. So first you just worry about questions, and then time, and finally strategy:

Success Strategy

1. Find a good source for practice tests.
2. If you are willing to make a larger time investment, consider using more than one study guide. Often the different approaches of multiple authors will help you "get" difficult concepts.
3. Take a practice test with no time constraints, with all study helps, "open book." Take your time with questions and focus on applying strategies.
4. Take a practice test with time constraints, with all guides, "open book."
5. Take a final practice test without open material and with time limits.

If you have time to take more practice tests, just repeat step 5. By gradually exposing yourself to the full rigors of the test environment, you will condition your mind to the stress of test day and maximize your success.

Secret Key #4 - Prepare, Don't Procrastinate

Let me state an obvious fact: if you take the test three times, you will probably get three different scores. This is due to the way you feel on test day, the level of preparedness you have, and the version of the test you see. Despite the test writers' claims to the contrary, some versions of the test WILL be easier for you than others.

Since your future depends so much on your score, you should maximize your chances of success. In order to maximize the likelihood of success, you've got to prepare in advance. This means taking practice tests and spending time learning the information and test taking strategies you will need to succeed.

Never go take the actual test as a "practice" test, expecting that you can just take it again if you need to. Take all the practice tests you can on your own, but when you go to take the official test, be prepared, be focused, and do your best the first time!

Secret Key #5 - Test Yourself

Everyone knows that time is money. There is no need to spend too much of your time or too little of your time preparing for the test. You should only spend as much of your precious time preparing as is necessary for you to get the score you need.

Once you have taken a practice test under real conditions of time constraints, then you will know if you are ready for the test or not.

If you have scored extremely high the first time that you take the practice test, then there is not much point in spending countless hours studying. You are already there.

Benchmark your abilities by retaking practice tests and seeing how much you have improved. Once you consistently score high enough to guarantee success, then you are ready.

If you have scored well below where you need, then knuckle down and begin studying in earnest. Check your improvement regularly through the use of practice tests under real conditions. Above all, don't worry, panic, or give up. The key is perseverance!

Then, when you go to take the test, remain confident and remember how well you did on the practice tests. If you can score high enough on a practice test, then you can do the same on the real thing.

General Strategies

The most important thing you can do is to ignore your fears and jump into the test immediately. Do not be overwhelmed by any strange-sounding terms. You have to jump into the test like jumping into a pool—all at once is the easiest way.

Make Predictions

As you read and understand the question, try to guess what the answer will be. Remember that several of the answer choices are wrong, and once you begin reading them, your mind will immediately become cluttered with answer choices designed to throw you off. Your mind is typically the most focused immediately after you have read the question and digested its contents. If you can, try to predict what the correct answer will be. You may be surprised at what you can predict.

Quickly scan the choices and see if your prediction is in the listed answer choices. If it is, then you can be quite confident that you have the right answer. It still won't hurt to check the other answer choices, but most of the time, you've got it!

Answer the Question

It may seem obvious to only pick answer choices that answer the question, but the test writers can create some excellent answer choices that are wrong. Don't pick an answer just because it sounds right, or you believe it to be true. It MUST answer the question. Once you've made your selection, always go back and check it against the question and make sure that you didn't misread the question and that the answer choice does answer the question posed.

Benchmark

After you read the first answer choice, decide if you think it sounds correct or not. If it doesn't, move on to the next answer choice. If it does, mentally mark that answer choice. This doesn't mean that you've definitely selected it as your answer choice, it just means that it's the best you've seen thus far. Go ahead and read the next choice. If the next choice is worse than the one you've already selected, keep going to the next answer choice. If the next choice is better than the choice you've already selected, mentally mark the new answer choice as your best guess.

The first answer choice that you select becomes your standard. Every other answer choice must be benchmarked against that standard. That choice is correct until proven otherwise by another answer choice beating it out. Once you've decided that no other answer choice seems as good, do one final check to ensure that your answer choice answers the question posed.

Valid Information

Don't discount any of the information provided in the question. Every piece of information may be necessary to determine the correct answer. None of the information in the question is there to throw you off (while the answer choices will certainly have information to throw you off). If two seemingly unrelated topics are discussed, don't ignore either. You can be confident there is a relationship, or it wouldn't be included in the question, and you are probably going to have to determine what is that relationship to find the answer.

Avoid "Fact Traps"

Don't get distracted by a choice that is factually true. Your search is for the answer that answers the question. Stay focused and don't fall for an answer that is true but irrelevant. Always go back to the question and make sure you're choosing an answer that actually answers the question and is not just a true statement. An answer can be factually correct, but it MUST answer the question asked. Additionally, two answers can both be seemingly correct, so be sure to read all of the answer choices, and make sure that you get the one that BEST answers the question.

Milk the Question

Some of the questions may throw you completely off. They might deal with a subject you have not been exposed to, or one that you haven't reviewed in years. While your lack of knowledge about the subject will be a hindrance, the question itself can give you many clues that will help you find the correct answer. Read the question carefully and look for clues. Watch particularly for adjectives and nouns describing difficult terms or words that you don't recognize. Regardless of whether you completely understand a word or not, replacing it with a synonym, either provided or one you more familiar with, may help you to understand what the questions are asking. Rather than wracking your mind about specific detailed information concerning a difficult term or word, try to use mental substitutes that are easier to understand.

The Trap of Familiarity

Don't just choose a word because you recognize it. On difficult questions, you may not recognize a number of words in the answer choices. The test writers don't put "make-believe" words on the test, so don't think that just because you only recognize all the words in one answer choice that that answer choice must be correct. If you only recognize words in one answer choice, then focus on that one. Is it correct? Try your best to determine if it is correct. If it is, that's great. If not, eliminate it. Each word and answer choice you eliminate increases your chances of getting the question correct, even if you then have to guess among the unfamiliar choices.

Eliminate Answers

Eliminate choices as soon as you realize they are wrong. But be careful! Make sure you consider all of the possible answer choices. Just because one appears right, doesn't mean that the next one won't be even better! The test writers will usually put more than one good answer choice for every question, so read all of them. Don't worry if you are stuck between two that seem right. By getting down to just two remaining possible choices, your odds are now 50/50. Rather than wasting too much time, play the odds. You are guessing, but guessing wisely because you've been able to knock out some of the answer choices that you know are wrong. If you are eliminating choices and realize that the last answer choice you are left with is also obviously wrong, don't panic. Start over and consider each choice again. There may easily be something that you missed the first time and will realize on the second pass.

Tough Questions

If you are stumped on a problem or it appears too hard or too difficult, don't waste time. Move on! Remember though, if you can quickly check for obviously incorrect answer choices, your chances of guessing correctly are greatly improved. Before you completely give up, at least try to knock out a couple of possible answers. Eliminate what you can and then guess at the remaining answer choices before moving on.

Brainstorm

If you get stuck on a difficult question, spend a few seconds quickly brainstorming. Run through the complete list of possible answer choices. Look at each choice and ask yourself, "Could this answer the question satisfactorily?" Go through each answer choice and consider it independently of the others. By systematically going through all possibilities, you may find something that you would otherwise overlook. Remember though that when you get stuck, it's important to try to keep moving.

Read Carefully

Understand the problem. Read the question and answer choices carefully. Don't miss the question because you misread the terms. You have plenty of time to read each question thoroughly and make sure you understand what is being asked. Yet a happy medium must be attained, so don't waste too much time. You must read carefully, but efficiently.

Face Value

When in doubt, use common sense. Always accept the situation in the problem at face value. Don't read too much into it. These problems will not require you to make huge leaps of logic. The test writers aren't trying to throw you off with a cheap trick. If you have to go beyond creativity and make a leap of logic in order to have an answer choice answer the question, then you should look at the other answer choices. Don't overcomplicate the problem by creating theoretical relationships or explanations that will warp time or space. These are normal problems rooted in reality. It's just that the applicable relationship or explanation may not be readily apparent and you have to figure things out. Use your common sense to interpret anything that isn't clear.

Prefixes

If you're having trouble with a word in the question or answer choices, try dissecting it. Take advantage of every clue that the word might include. Prefixes and suffixes can be a huge help. Usually they allow you to determine a basic meaning. Pre- means before, post- means after, pro - is positive, de- is negative. From these prefixes and suffixes, you can get an idea of the general meaning of the word and try to put it into context. Beware though of any traps. Just because con- is the opposite of pro-, doesn't necessarily mean congress is the opposite of progress!

Hedge Phrases

Watch out for critical hedge phrases, led off with words such as "likely," "may," "can," "sometimes," "often," "almost," "mostly," "usually," "generally," "rarely," and "sometimes." Question writers insert these hedge phrases to cover every possibility. Often an answer choice will be wrong simply because it leaves no room for exception. Unless the situation calls for them, avoid answer choices that have definitive words like "exactly," and "always."

Switchback Words

Stay alert for "switchbacks." These are the words and phrases frequently used to alert you to shifts in thought. The most common switchback word is "but." Others include "although," "however," "nevertheless," "on the other hand," "even though," "while," "in spite of," "despite," and "regardless of."

New Information

Correct answer choices will rarely have completely new information included. Answer choices typically are straightforward reflections of the material asked about and will directly relate to the question. If a new piece of information is included in an answer choice that doesn't even seem to relate to the topic being asked about, then that answer choice is likely incorrect. All of the information needed to answer the question is usually provided for you in the question. You should not have to make guesses that are unsupported or choose answer choices that require unknown information that cannot be reasoned from what is given.

Time Management

On technical questions, don't get lost on the technical terms. Don't spend too much time on any one question. If you don't know what a term means, then odds are you aren't going to get much further since you don't have a dictionary. You should be able to immediately recognize whether or not you know a term. If you don't, work with the other clues that you have—the other answer choices and terms provided—but don't waste too much time trying to figure out a difficult term that you don't know.

Contextual Clues

Look for contextual clues. An answer can be right but not the correct answer. The contextual clues will help you find the answer that is most right and is correct. Understand the context in which a phrase or statement is made. This will help you make important distinctions.

Don't Panic

Panicking will not answer any questions for you; therefore, it isn't helpful. When you first see the question, if your mind goes blank, take a deep breath. Force yourself to mechanically go through the steps of solving the problem using the strategies you've learned.

Pace Yourself

Don't get clock fever. It's easy to be overwhelmed when you're looking at a page full of questions, your mind is full of random thoughts and feeling confused, and the clock is ticking down faster than you would like. Calm down and maintain the pace that you have set for yourself. As long as you are on track by monitoring your pace, you are guaranteed to have enough time for yourself. When you get to the last few minutes of the test, it may seem like you won't have enough time left, but if you only have as many questions as you should have left at that point, then you're right on track!

Answer Selection

The best way to pick an answer choice is to eliminate all of those that are wrong, until only one is left and confirm that is the correct answer. Sometimes though, an answer choice may immediately look right. Be careful! Take a second to make sure that the other choices are not equally obvious. Don't make a hasty mistake. There are only two times that you should stop before checking other answers. First is when you are positive that the answer choice you have selected is correct. Second is when time is almost out and you have to make a quick guess!

Check Your Work

Since you will probably not know every term listed and the answer to every question, it is important that you get credit for the ones that you do know. Don't miss any questions through careless mistakes. If at all possible, try to take a second to look back over your answer selection and make sure you've selected the correct answer choice and haven't made a costly careless mistake (such as marking an answer choice that you didn't mean to mark). The time it takes for this quick double check should more than pay for itself in caught mistakes.

Beware of Directly Quoted Answers

Sometimes an answer choice will repeat word for word a portion of the question or reference section. However, beware of such exact duplication. It may be a trap! More than likely, the correct choice will paraphrase or summarize a point, rather than being exactly the same wording.

Slang

Scientific sounding answers are better than slang ones. An answer choice that begins "To compare the outcomes..." is much more likely to be correct than one that begins "Because some people insisted..."

Extreme Statements

Avoid wild answers that throw out highly controversial ideas that are proclaimed as established fact. An answer choice that states the "process should used in certain situations, if..." is much more likely to be correct than one that states the "process should be discontinued completely." The first is a calm rational statement and doesn't even make a definitive, uncompromising stance, using a hedge word "if" to provide wiggle room, whereas the second choice is a radical idea and far more extreme.

Answer Choice Families

When you have two or more answer choices that are direct opposites or parallels, one of them is usually the correct answer. For instance, if one answer choice states "x increases" and another answer choice states "x decreases" or "y increases," then those two or three answer choices are very similar in construction and fall into the same family of answer choices. A family of answer choices consists of two or three answer choices, very similar in construction, but often with directly opposite meanings. Usually the correct answer choice will be in that family of answer choices. The "odd man out" or answer choice that doesn't seem to fit the parallel construction of the other answer choices is more likely to be incorrect.

Special Report: How to Overcome Test Anxiety

The very nature of tests caters to some level of anxiety, nervousness, or tension, just as we feel for any important event that occurs in our lives. A little bit of anxiety or nervousness can be a good thing. It helps us with motivation, and makes achievement just that much sweeter. However, too much anxiety can be a problem, especially if it hinders our ability to function and perform.

"Test anxiety," is the term that refers to the emotional reactions that some test-takers experience when faced with a test or exam. Having a fear of testing and exams is based upon a rational fear, since the test-taker's performance can shape the course of an academic career. Nevertheless, experiencing excessive fear of examinations will only interfere with the test-taker's ability to perform and chance to be successful.

There are a large variety of causes that can contribute to the development and sensation of test anxiety. These include, but are not limited to, lack of preparation and worrying about issues surrounding the test.

Lack of Preparation

Lack of preparation can be identified by the following behaviors or situations:

Not scheduling enough time to study, and therefore cramming the night before the test or exam
Managing time poorly, to create the sensation that there is not enough time to do everything
Failing to organize the text information in advance, so that the study material consists of the entire text and not simply the pertinent information
Poor overall studying habits

Worrying, on the other hand, can be related to both the test taker, or many other factors around him/her that will be affected by the results of the test. These include worrying about:

Previous performances on similar exams, or exams in general
How friends and other students are achieving
The negative consequences that will result from a poor grade or failure

There are three primary elements to test anxiety. Physical components, which involve the same typical bodily reactions as those to acute anxiety (to be discussed below). Emotional factors have to do with fear or panic. Mental or cognitive issues concerning attention spans and memory abilities.

Physical Signals

There are many different symptoms of test anxiety, and these are not limited to mental and emotional strain. Frequently there are a range of physical signals that will let a test taker know that he/she is suffering from test anxiety. These bodily changes can include the following:

Perspiring
Sweaty palms
Wet, trembling hands
Nausea
Dry mouth
A knot in the stomach
Headache
Faintness
Muscle tension
Aching shoulders, back and neck
Rapid heart beat
Feeling too hot/cold

To recognize the sensation of test anxiety, a test-taker should monitor him/herself for the following sensations:

The physical distress symptoms as listed above
Emotional sensitivity, expressing emotional feelings such as the need to cry or laugh too much, or a sensation of anger or helplessness
A decreased ability to think, causing the test-taker to blank out or have racing thoughts that are hard to organize or control.

Though most students will feel some level of anxiety when faced with a test or exam, the majority can cope with that anxiety and maintain it at a manageable level. However, those who cannot are faced with a very real and very serious condition, which can and should be controlled for the immeasurable benefit of this sufferer.

Naturally, these sensations lead to negative results for the testing experience. The most common effects of test anxiety have to do with nervousness and mental blocking.

Nervousness

Nervousness can appear in several different levels:

The test-taker's difficulty, or even inability to read and understand the questions on the test
The difficulty or inability to organize thoughts to a coherent form
The difficulty or inability to recall key words and concepts relating to the testing questions (especially essays)
The receipt of poor grades on a test, though the test material was well known by the test taker

Conversely, a person may also experience mental blocking, which involves:

Blanking out on test questions
Only remembering the correct answers to the questions when the test has already finished.

Fortunately for test anxiety sufferers, beating these feelings, to a large degree, has to do with proper preparation. When a test taker has a feeling of preparedness, then anxiety will be dramatically lessened.

The first step to resolving anxiety issues is to distinguish which of the two types of anxiety are being suffered. If the anxiety is a direct result of a lack of preparation, this should be considered a normal reaction, and the anxiety level (as opposed to the test results) shouldn't be anything to worry about. However, if, when adequately prepared, the test-taker still panics, blanks out, or seems to overreact, this is not a fully rational reaction. While this can be considered normal too, there are many ways to combat and overcome these effects.

Remember that anxiety cannot be entirely eliminated, however, there are ways to minimize it, to make the anxiety easier to manage. Preparation is one of the best ways to minimize test anxiety. Therefore the following techniques are wise in order to best fight off any anxiety that may want to build.

To begin with, try to avoid cramming before a test, whenever it is possible. By trying to memorize an entire term's worth of information in one day, you'll be shocking your system, and not giving yourself a very good chance to absorb the information. This is an easy path to anxiety, so for those who suffer from test anxiety, cramming should not even be considered an option.

Instead of cramming, work throughout the semester to combine all of the material which is presented throughout the semester, and work on it gradually as the course goes by, making sure to master the main concepts first, leaving minor details for a week or so before the test.

To study for the upcoming exam, be sure to pose questions that may be on the examination, to gauge the ability to answer them by integrating the ideas from your texts, notes and lectures, as well as any supplementary readings.

If it is truly impossible to cover all of the information that was covered in that particular term, concentrate on the most important portions, that can be covered very well. Learn these concepts as best as possible, so that when the test comes, a goal can be made to use these concepts as presentations of your knowledge.

In addition to study habits, changes in attitude are critical to beating a struggle with test anxiety. In fact, an improvement of the perspective over the entire test-taking experience can actually help a test taker to enjoy studying and therefore improve the overall experience. Be certain not to overemphasize the significance of the grade - know that the result of the test is neither a reflection of self worth, nor is it a measure of intelligence; one grade will not predict a person's future success.

To improve an overall testing outlook, the following steps should be tried:

Keeping in mind that the most reasonable expectation for taking a test is to expect to try to demonstrate as much of what you know as you possibly can.
Reminding ourselves that a test is only one test; this is not the only one, and there will be others.
The thought of thinking of oneself in an irrational, all-or-nothing term should be avoided at all costs.
A reward should be designated for after the test, so there's something to look forward to. Whether it be going to a movie, going out to eat, or simply visiting friends, schedule it in advance, and do it no matter what result is expected on the exam.

Test-takers should also keep in mind that the basics are some of the most important things, even beyond anti-anxiety techniques and studying. Never neglect the basic social, emotional and biological needs, in order to try to absorb information. In order to best achieve, these three factors must be held as just as important as the studying itself.

Study Steps

Remember the following important steps for studying:

Maintain healthy nutrition and exercise habits. Continue both your recreational activities and social pass times. These both contribute to your physical and emotional well being.
Be certain to get a good amount of sleep, especially the night before the test, because when you're overtired you are not able to perform to the best of your best ability.
Keep the studying pace to a moderate level by taking breaks when they are needed, and varying the work whenever possible, to keep the mind fresh instead of getting bored. When enough studying has been done that all the material that can be learned has been learned, and the test taker is prepared for the test, stop studying and do something relaxing such as listening to music, watching a movie, or taking a warm bubble bath.

There are also many other techniques to minimize the uneasiness or apprehension that is experienced along with test anxiety before, during, or even after the examination. In fact, there are a great deal of things that can be done to stop anxiety from interfering with lifestyle and performance. Again, remember that anxiety will not be eliminated entirely, and it shouldn't be. Otherwise that "up" feeling for exams would not exist, and most of us depend on that sensation to perform better than usual. However, this anxiety has to be at a level that is manageable.

Of course, as we have just discussed, being prepared for the exam is half the battle right away. Attending all classes, finding out what knowledge will be expected on the exam, and knowing the exam schedules are easy steps to lowering anxiety. Keeping up with work will remove the need to cram, and efficient study habits will eliminate wasted time. Studying should be done in an ideal location for concentration, so that it is simple to become interested in the material and give it complete attention. A method such as SQ3R (Survey, Question, Read, Recite, Review) is a wonderful key to follow to make sure that the study habits are as effective as possible, especially in the case of learning from a

- 139 -

textbook. Flashcards are great techniques for memorization. Learning to take good notes will mean that notes will be full of useful information, so that less sifting will need to be done to seek out what is pertinent for studying. Reviewing notes after class and then again on occasion will keep the information fresh in the mind. From notes that have been taken summary sheets and outlines can be made for simpler reviewing.

A study group can also be a very motivational and helpful place to study, as there will be a sharing of ideas, all of the minds can work together, to make sure that everyone understands, and the studying will be made more interesting because it will be a social occasion.

Basically, though, as long as the test-taker remains organized and self confident, with efficient study habits, less time will need to be spent studying, and higher grades will be achieved.

To become self confident, there are many useful steps. The first of these is "self talk." It has been shown through extensive research, that self-talk for students who suffer from test anxiety, should be well monitored, in order to make sure that it contributes to self confidence as opposed to sinking the student. Frequently the self talk of test-anxious students is negative or self-defeating, thinking that everyone else is smarter and faster, that they always mess up, and that if they don't do well, they'll fail the entire course. It is important to decreasing anxiety that awareness is made of self talk. Try writing any negative self thoughts and then disputing them with a positive statement instead. Begin self-encouragement as though it was a friend speaking. Repeat positive statements to help reprogram the mind to believing in successes instead of failures.

Helpful Techniques

Other extremely helpful techniques include:

Self-visualization of doing well and reaching goals
While aiming for an "A" level of understanding, don't try to "overprotect" by setting your expectations lower. This will only convince the mind to stop studying in order to meet the lower expectations.
Don't make comparisons with the results or habits of other students. These are individual factors, and different things work for different people, causing different results.
Strive to become an expert in learning what works well, and what can be done in order to improve. Consider collecting this data in a journal.
Create rewards for after studying instead of doing things before studying that will only turn into avoidance behaviors.
Make a practice of relaxing - by using methods such as progressive relaxation, self-hypnosis, guided imagery, etc - in order to make relaxation an automatic sensation.
Work on creating a state of relaxed concentration so that concentrating will take on the focus of the mind, so that none will be wasted on worrying.
Take good care of the physical self by eating well and getting enough sleep.
Plan in time for exercise and stick to this plan.

Beyond these techniques, there are other methods to be used before, during and after the test that will help the test-taker perform well in addition to overcoming anxiety.

Before the exam comes the academic preparation. This involves establishing a study schedule and beginning at least one week before the actual date of the test. By doing this, the anxiety of not having enough time to study for the test will be automatically eliminated. Moreover, this will make the studying a much more effective experience, ensuring that the learning will be an easier process. This relieves much undue pressure on the test-taker.

Summary sheets, note cards, and flash cards with the main concepts and examples of these main concepts should be prepared in advance of the actual studying time. A topic should never be eliminated from this process. By omitting a topic because it isn't expected to be on the test is only setting up the test-taker for anxiety should it actually appear on the exam. Utilize the course syllabus for laying out the topics that should be studied. Carefully go over the notes that were made in class, paying special attention to any of the issues that the professor took special care to emphasize while lecturing in class. In the textbooks, use the chapter review, or if possible, the chapter tests, to begin your review.

It may even be possible to ask the instructor what information will be covered on the exam, or what the format of the exam will be (for example, multiple choice, essay, free form, true-false). Additionally, see if it is possible to find out how many questions will be on the test. If a review sheet or sample test has been offered by the professor, make good use of it, above anything else, for the preparation for the test. Another great resource for getting to know the examination is reviewing tests from previous semesters. Use these tests to review, and aim to achieve a 100% score on each of the possible topics. With a few exceptions, the goal that you set for yourself is the highest one that you will reach.

Take all of the questions that were assigned as homework, and rework them to any other possible course material. The more problems reworked, the more skill and confidence will form as a result. When forming the solution to a problem, write out each of the steps. Don't simply do head work. By doing as many steps on paper as possible, much clarification and therefore confidence will be formed. Do this with as many homework problems as possible, before checking the answers. By checking the answer after each problem, a reinforcement will exist, that will not be on the exam. Study situations should be as exam-like as possible, to prime the test-taker's system for the experience. By waiting to check the answers at the end, a psychological advantage will be formed, to decrease the stress factor.

Another fantastic reason for not cramming is the avoidance of confusion in concepts, especially when it comes to mathematics. 8-10 hours of study will become one hundred percent more effective if it is spread out over a week or at least several days, instead of doing it all in one sitting. Recognize that the human brain requires time in order to assimilate new material, so frequent breaks and a span of study time over several days will be much more beneficial.

Additionally, don't study right up until the point of the exam. Studying should stop a minimum of one hour before the exam begins. This allows the brain to rest and put things in their proper order. This will also provide the time to become as relaxed as possible when going into the examination room. The test-taker will also have time to eat well and eat sensibly. Know that the brain needs food as much as the rest of the body. With enough food and enough sleep, as well as a relaxed attitude, the body and the mind are primed for success.

Avoid any anxious classmates who are talking about the exam. These students only spread anxiety, and are not worth sharing the anxious sentimentalities.

Before the test also involves creating a positive attitude, so mental preparation should also be a point of concentration. There are many keys to creating a positive attitude. Should fears become rushing in, make a visualization of taking the exam, doing well, and seeing an A written on the paper. Write out a list of affirmations that will bring a feeling of confidence, such as "I am doing well in my English class," "I studied well and know my material," "I enjoy this class." Even if the affirmations aren't believed at first, it sends a positive message to the subconscious which will result in an alteration of the overall belief system, which is the system that creates reality.

If a sensation of panic begins, work with the fear and imagine the very worst! Work through the entire scenario of not passing the test, failing the entire course, and dropping out of school, followed by not getting a job, and pushing a shopping cart through the dark alley where you'll live. This will place things into perspective! Then, practice deep breathing and create a visualization of the opposite situation - achieving an "A" on the exam, passing the entire course, receiving the degree at a graduation ceremony.

On the day of the test, there are many things to be done to ensure the best results, as well as the most calm outlook. The following stages are suggested in order to maximize test-taking potential:

Begin the examination day with a moderate breakfast, and avoid any coffee or beverages with caffeine if the test taker is prone to jitters. Even people who are used to managing caffeine can feel jittery or light-headed when it is taken on a test day.
Attempt to do something that is relaxing before the examination begins. As last minute cramming clouds the mastering of overall concepts, it is better to use this time to create a calming outlook.
Be certain to arrive at the test location well in advance, in order to provide time to select a location that is away from doors, windows and other distractions, as well as giving enough time to relax before the test begins.
Keep away from anxiety generating classmates who will upset the sensation of stability and relaxation that is being attempted before the exam.
Should the waiting period before the exam begins cause anxiety, create a self-distraction by reading a light magazine or something else that is relaxing and simple.

During the exam itself, read the entire exam from beginning to end, and find out how much time should be allotted to each individual problem. Once writing the exam, should more time be taken for a problem, it should be abandoned, in order to begin another problem. If there is time at the end, the unfinished problem can always be returned to and completed.

Read the instructions very carefully - twice - so that unpleasant surprises won't follow during or after the exam has ended.

When writing the exam, pretend that the situation is actually simply the completion of homework within a library, or at home. This will assist in forming a relaxed atmosphere, and will allow the brain extra focus for the complex thinking function.

Begin the exam with all of the questions with which the most confidence is felt. This will build the confidence level regarding the entire exam and will begin a quality momentum. This will also create encouragement for trying the problems where uncertainty resides.

Going with the "gut instinct" is always the way to go when solving a problem. Second guessing should be avoided at all costs. Have confidence in the ability to do well.

For essay questions, create an outline in advance that will keep the mind organized and make certain that all of the points are remembered. For multiple choice, read every answer, even if the correct one has been spotted - a better one may exist.

Continue at a pace that is reasonable and not rushed, in order to be able to work carefully. Provide enough time to go over the answers at the end, to check for small errors that can be corrected.

Should a feeling of panic begin, breathe deeply, and think of the feeling of the body releasing sand through its pores. Visualize a calm, peaceful place, and include all of the sights, sounds and sensations of this image. Continue the deep breathing, and take a few minutes to continue this with closed eyes. When all is well again, return to the test.

If a "blanking" occurs for a certain question, skip it and move on to the next question. There will be time to return to the other question later. Get everything done that can be done, first, to guarantee all the grades that can be compiled, and to build all of the confidence possible. Then return to the weaker questions to build the marks from there.

Remember, one's own reality can be created, so as long as the belief is there, success will follow. And remember: anxiety can happen later, right now, there's an exam to be written!

After the examination is complete, whether there is a feeling for a good grade or a bad grade, don't dwell on the exam, and be certain to follow through on the reward that was promised...and enjoy it! Don't dwell on any mistakes that have been made, as there is nothing that can be done at this point anyway.

Additionally, don't begin to study for the next test right away. Do something relaxing for a while, and let the mind relax and prepare itself to begin absorbing information again.

From the results of the exam - both the grade and the entire experience, be certain to learn from what has gone on. Perfect studying habits and work some more on confidence in order to make the next examination experience even better than the last one.

Learn to avoid places where openings occurred for laziness, procrastination and day dreaming.

Use the time between this exam and the next one to better learn to relax, even learning to relax on cue, so that any anxiety can be controlled during the next exam. Learn how to relax the body. Slouch in your chair if that helps. Tighten and then relax all of the different muscle groups, one group at a time, beginning with the feet and then working all the way up to the neck and face. This will ultimately relax the muscles more than they were to begin with. Learn how to breathe deeply and comfortably, and focus on this breathing going in and out as a relaxing thought. With every exhale, repeat the word "relax."

As common as test anxiety is, it is very possible to overcome it. Make yourself one of the test-takers who overcome this frustrating hindrance.

Special Report: Additional Bonus Material

Due to our efforts to try to keep this book to a manageable length, we've created a link that will give you access to all of your additional bonus material.

Please visit http://www.mometrix.com/bonus948/certpaypro to access the information.